Creative
Person and
Creative Process

Creative
Person and
Creative Process

Frank Barron

Institute of Personality Assessment and Research
University of California, Berkeley

Holt, Rinehart and Winston, Inc.
New York   Chicago   San Francisco   Atlanta
Dallas   Montreal   Toronto   London   Sydney

*To my daughters, Brigid Jessica Sarah
and Anthea Rose,
and to their fond grandparents,
Charles and Jessie Camp*

Copyright © 1969 by Holt, Rinehart and Winston, Inc.
All rights reserved
Library of Congress Catalog Card Number: 76-75918
SBN: 03-080971-1
Printed in the United States of America
9 8 7 6 5 4 3 2 1

Preface

The setting for much of the work reported in this book has been the Institute of Personality Assessment and Research, a division of the University of California at Berkeley. The method of study employed there was originally not a research method at all. Rather, as the word *assessment* implies, it was a way of appraising persons, or of judging whether a person could meet the requirements of a particular job. It did this by a combination of interviews, situational tests presumably calling for the exercise of the qualities the job required, and standardized questionnaires and projective techniques.

These procedures of assessment were knit together in an unusual way, however, for the most important aspect of the research method is the personal relationship established between the subjects of study and the "assessors." The creative people who accepted invitations to be studied were not by any means passive objects of observation. My own study of writers reported in this volume included many who have made a mark not just by writing but also through the impact of their personalities;

among those who have been publicly identified, by themselves or others, as taking part in the study were Truman Capote, Norman Mailer, MacKinlay Kantor, Frank O'Connor, and Kenneth Rexroth, none of whom sat still to be studied. The research engaged creative persons in a process that was itself often quite creative. Some surprising insights developed spontaneously in the course of the meetings and interviews.

This way of doing research reflects the basic emphasis in my own approach to the study of creativity. I am concerned with *persons* and with *process* as they relate to one another in psychic creation. In the creative person one can clearly see at work the forces and forms that characterize the creative process in general. Indeed, a person is a form in process, and the evolution of the self in a creative person is an instance of the creative process in nature. Relationships between persons also may set the creative process in motion.

Such is the thesis and theme of this book. Person and process are the focus of attention. I have tried to take account as well of the recent extensive efforts at measurement of factors that are to be found in creative thinking and in creative personal behavior, but my approach remains essentially intuitive and introspective even while it makes use of psychometrics and objective methods as much as possible. We may measure states and traits fairly well but if our interest is in the development of human form and the evolution of mind, we must let ourselves enter into relationship with the observed as freely as we can. Indeed, if research on creativity is itself a creative force and a part of the creative movement of mind in our own time, as I believe it is, we cannot do otherwise.

Although I am writing as a psychologist and educator and with the hope that other psychologists and educators will find something of professional value in this book, I have chosen a more discursive and informal style than is usual in professional writing. I have done so in part because I have already reported, in appropriate technical detail, many of my own studies that I discuss again here. What I am doing now is approaching the subject more impressionistically, hoping thereby to communicate more of the meaning of this work to the general reader, and especially to the psychologically minded student and teacher in diverse fields of specialization.

The book itself is based upon my essay in *New Directions in Psychology II* (Barron *et al.*, 1965), also published by Holt, Rinehart and Winston. I have added much new material, both from the professional literature and from my own previously unpublished studies (such as the research on originality and innovation in business enterprises and on the heritability of creativity using the classical twin method). I have also broadened the discussion of educational techniques for helping to develop creativity and have provided an additional chapter on the development of the self in the creative person. This latter is an extension of my monograph *An Eye More Fantastical* (Barron, 1967), published in the Viktor Lowenfeld Monograph Series by the National Art Education Association. The final chapter is an abridgment of my essay "Diffusion, Integration, and Enduring Attention in the Creative Process" (White, ed., *The Study of Lives*, New York: Atherton, 1963).

As I hope the book makes plain, I owe a large debt of gratitude to the staff of the Institute of Personality Assessment and Research, not only for permission to draw material from researches for which particular staff members are responsible, but also for the contributions of its members as assessors in many of my own studies and for their suggestions concerning revision of the manuscript. Those who have participated in the work include Donald W. MacKinnon, Director of the Institute; Richard S. Crutchfield, Associate Director; and Harrison Gough, Ravenna Helson, Wallace B. Hall, Kenneth Craik, and Susan Hopkins, staff members.

The influence of John W. Gardner in encouraging the initial phases of the program of research on creativity at the Institute deserves special mention. The program grew out of a proposal centering upon the question of originality that I had written in 1954 for informal consideration by the Carnegie Corporation of New York. Dr. Gardner himself (then president at Carnegie) suggested that the topic be broadened and that we study highly creative people, seeking clues in their lives and personalities to the nature of the creative process and to conditions that facilitate creative personal growth and achievement. This suggestion no doubt grew out of his own concern with personal excellence and self-renewal, topics upon which he later wrote the two thoughtful books that have so influenced American education (*Excellence: Can we be equal and excellent too?* New York: Harper & Row, 1961; *Self-renewal: The individual and the innovative society.* New York: Harper & Row, 1963). The Carnegie Corporation supported the Institute's work financially for a period of ten years, and it is with great pleasure that I here acknowledge that contribution as well as the role Dr. Gardner personally played in getting the research going.

Generous assistance in test scoring, data analysis, and preparation of manuscripts was provided over the years by more than one hundred research assistants and clerical workers, who go unnamed but are remembered here. Of particular importance to the research program, however, were two secretaries who deserve a special vote of thanks for their personal kindness and patience, Eve Louis and Florence Cho.

Finally, to the subjects of study, in our own work as well as that of others, we wish to express our gratitude. Without the cooperation of people, the research psychologist in the field of human personality can offer nothing in the way of objective facts.

F. B.

Berkeley, California
January 10, 1969

Contents

Creative
Person and
Creative Process

Introduction

There is a rapidly growing core of educators and educational programs throughout the United States dedicated to creativity as the most important goal of education. This movement, beginning formally in psychological and educational research in 1950 but rooted in massive social forces set in motion with the conclusion of World War II, has proliferated in education proper since 1960 and has taken quite diverse forms. The programs range from the intellectually rather far out but interesting melange at Esalen Institute on the Pacific Coast to the pragmatic and industry-oriented centers devoted to invention and problem solving, such as the Creative Education Foundation in New York and the Synectics group in Massachusetts. There is increasing communication among these programs, aided both by interested private foundations (notably the Carnegie Corporation and the Richardson Foundation) and by the U. S. Office of Education.

There have been obstacles and resistances to the spread of this special approach, as might be expected. Inertia in the educational establishment itself has provided part of the resistance. The existence of other formidable problems has claimed the attention of educational leaders, to whom "creativity" seems a luxury that can wait till better times.

Then, too, there is the enemy within: the temptation on the part of those genuinely interested in creativity as an educational goal to seek in techniques and pedagogical devices a packaged method for stimulating creative processes; the invitation from eager, good-hearted "converts" to accept easy clichés about creativity and its blessings and to forget about the thorn that goes with the rose (if it is a rose); and the inevitable doubts that come with realization that success has been only partial or ephemeral. There is also a tendency for any concerted effort that becomes a "movement" to take too seriously the singularity of its own vision and to be either messianic or precious. I have often had occasion to recall the reaction of MacKinlay Kantor, one of the writers who took part in my own research on creative writing. At the conclusion of the three days of psychological "assessment," when all of us were saying goodbye to one another, he remarked that he had found, somewhat to his surprise, that the psychologists conducting the study were a likeable and worthwhile bunch; but, he added, he could not understand why we were not engaged in equally worthwhile work, such as flood relief.

This feeling that psychological research on creativity, and educational efforts to increase it, may not really be sound or substantial has been expressed by many observers, and with some reason. The allure, as distinguished from the genuine force, of some of the more esoteric educational techniques that have been developed to enhance creativity can be traced, in part at least, to the peculiarly American faith in gadgetry and the application of new forms of energy to speed things up and get the job done. I believe it was Arthur Koestler who coined the term "instant Zen" to describe the goal, as he saw it, of the early users of LSD among the mystical cults that flourished in southern California in the 1950's. That goal seemed to be a quick and easy throughway to the spiritual mountaintop. To a European artist, bred on exacting discipline and high standards of technical command in music, painting, and literature—not to mention asceticism, disciplined meditation, and self-control in the religious life—the idea that the way to philosophy or art might lie through drugs was almost sacrilegious. And that there could be educational techniques which depended little or not at all upon training in the *content* of a given discipline, and yet succeeded in freeing the mental processes for creative thinking, was equally repugnant. "Instant creativity" seemed to be the goal of this new brand of educational evangelism.

Koestler has assembled a considerable body of evidence in his monumental tome *The Act of Creation* to support the view that great insights, results of what he calls the "bisociative process," occur only in minds that are amply prepared, through saturation in the relevant scholarly or artistic disciplines, to see hidden connections. You have to know a lot about the old to see the new. Although one's education may be unconventional—and certainly in our own studies we have seen that creative individuals frequently reject the schools and teach themselves—it remains true that hard work and dedicated practice are the almost invariable precursors of original and distinctive achievement.

Koestler wrote as an historian of ideas and a scholar in the general area of intellectual biography. But in the United States, measurement-based research on creativity as a general topic has been increasing exponentially since 1950. In what is recognized in retrospect as the crucial professional impetus to research in this field, Dr. J. P. Guilford in his parting address as president of the American Psychological Association (1950) pointed out that up to that time only 186 out of 121,000 topics listed in *Psychological Abstracts* dealt with creative imagination. By the time of the first national conference on creativity sponsored by the National Science Foundation at the University of Utah, in 1956, this number had doubled. By 1962, when *Scientific Creativity* (C. W. Taylor and F. Barron, eds.) went to press with a summary of the first three biennial Utah–NSF conferences, approximately 400 references appearing since 1950 were available for citation. In 1964, the comprehensive bibliography published by the Creative

Education Foundation listed 515 items, most of which had appeared since 1960. In the most recent bibliography of the Foundation, including papers given at the 1965 meetings of the American Psychological Association, 4176 references were listed, nearly 3000 of them dated later than 1950.

Courses in creative thinking also are multiplying rapidly. Research on creativity has found application especially in such centers as the University of Buffalo, the University of Minnesota, the University of Utah, Macalester College, Wayne State University, and Drake University, where regular courses in creative problem solving are offered. Many psychology departments offer courses and seminars on creativity. Adult education centers have also been responsive to demand from adults for work on creativity, and the National Association of Public Adult Educators has recently sponsored a book titled *How to Be a More Creative Adult Learner*. Many business organizations are offering such courses for their employees; these include corporations such as General Electric, U. S. Steel, General Motors, Westinghouse, and Bell Telephone, all of whom are highly dependent on innovativeness in their professional personnel. The military services and the U. S. Veterans Administration have also sponsored workshops, conferences, and in-service training for creative thinking.

The rapid increase in knowledge about creativity, and the flood of new research and theoretical formulations, led the Creative Education Foundation in 1967 to launch a new professional journal, *The Journal of Creative Behavior*. The journal is published quarterly, and its immediate success in finding more than 5000 professional subscribers in its first year of publication testifies to its timeliness. It is at present the best single source of information concerning most recent developments in an area of research which now deserves recognition as a distinct field within psychology and education.

This remarkable surge of interest in research and training in creative thinking occurred, it is fair to say, not simply as a movement within the educational and psychological professions, but as part of a generally recognized social need for more information about positive aspects of human nature.

The end of the first half of the twentieth century had seen the profession of psychology well furnished with tests of "intelligence" but as yet poorly furnished with tests of that aspect of intelligence we call creativity. But the conclusion of World War II had left a number of psychologists with the conviction that efforts at measurement were badly needed in such trait areas as flexibility, initiative, ingenuity, adaptability, spontaneity, and originality. The psychologists who headed testing and selection programs in branches or special arms of the military establishment, such as the U. S. Air Corps and the Office of Strategic Services, returned to their academic positions with the determination to do something about the research lag in this whole set of valued human potentialities. Many other psychologists were feeling the same stir, and by 1951 several important research programs were in full swing.

J. P. Guilford had directed the Air Corps research on the selection of combat crews and, as we have said, he launched much of this new effort with his address as retiring president of the American Psychological Association in September, 1950. In that address he systematically surveyed the gaps in knowledge in the domain of intellectual abilities and listed dozens of new tests he and his colleagues in the Psychological Laboratory of the University of Southern California were then developing. He addressed himself to the topic with a certain amount of diffidence, beginning with these words: "I discuss the subject of creativity with considerable hesitation, for it represents an area in which psychologists, whether they be angels or not, have feared to tread."

My own work in creativity had begun quite independently of Guilford, two years earlier, and from a very different starting point. I had interested myself in the creative process in psychotherapy, viewed as an encounter of *persons* through whose meeting an interpersonal process was set in motion. This process might be a creative one, affecting both patient and therapist in significant ways. My goal was to describe the conditions under which the psychotherapeutic process proved creative, and to try to predict such creative outcomes (Barron, 1950).

This concern with person and process in creativity has characterized all my subsequent work at the Institute of Personality Assessment and Research, which had meanwhile been established at the University of California in Berkeley. The Institute was under the direction of Donald W. MacKinnon and Nevitt Sanford, both former students of Henry A. Murray at Harvard and collaborators with him on the germinal *Explorations in Personality* (1938). The Institute's work centered upon the theme of "personal effectiveness," and originality was conceived to be one facet of this accomplishment.

At about this same time, John Flanagan, through the critical incident technique, was establishing the basis for his later comprehensive testing programs; most relevant in the present context was his development of performance tests of ingenuity, which combined open-endedness with mechanical scoring (1963). Murray himself, at Harvard, had already contributed an important instrument of observation in the study of imagination, the Thematic Apperception Test (1943), and students of his now set to work on studies of the creative process in poetry and the arts. L. L. Thurstone's influence continued to be felt, both through his own writings (1952) and the writings and organizational activities of his colleagues.

Especially noteworthy was the role of Calvin W. Taylor, then in charge of the fellowship program of the National Science Foundation and presently director of a very active program of research in creativity at the University of Utah. Taylor's importance in the definition of this research area has come not only through his research but also through his organization of national conferences of researchers, his establishment of effective lines of communication among them, and his periodic issuance of reports on progress.

A welcome contribution from another source was the clinically oriented studies of Ann Roe, who brought a depth-psychology approach to the study of imagery and motivation in creative artists and scientists. By the time of Guilford's 1950 address, she had already begun her pioneer researches in the study of scientific creativity that resulted in her 1952 book, *The Making of a Scientist*. By continuing the study of the same scientists in their later lives, she has been able to give an unusually full picture of temporal changes in productivity, the subject of a report she made at the 1967 Utah Conference on Creativity.

In the field of educational research, E. Paul Torrance at the University of Minnesota became the driving force behind a wide-ranging program of action-oriented studies in the elementary schools, with an emphasis on classroom conditions and school environments that affect creative development. Robert Burkhart, who with Kenneth Beittel has carried forth the spirit and advanced the ideas of Viktor Lowenfeld, made a significant contribution with his 1961 book, *Spontaneous and Deliberate Ways of Learning*. Elizabeth Starkweather at the University of Oklahoma and Elizabeth Drews at Michigan State University have done notably original work themselves with children and adolescents. Finally, J. W. Getzels and P. O. Jackson at the University of Chicago contributed some challenging data and observations on the relationship of creativity to intelligence in their studies of schoolchildren.

But the proliferation of research on creativity and of educational programs designed to enhance it has, as we have indicated, been remarkable in recent years, and it would be impossible for us to recognize here individually the thousands of psychologists and educators now involved in this effort in the United States. That it is a significant social and educational movement and is a manifestation of deeper forces in the culture itself seems apparent.

The nature of those deeper forces must concern us all as members of society. When as Americans we look at our own culture we see a not very united United States, a country of enormous vitality that is nonetheless deeply troubled by its own potential for violence. We must face the fact that as a nation we are armed to the teeth, with little guns and with big ones. The problem of social control of our own great force presents us as a people with an unprecedented responsibility.

The role of creativity in the whole process of socialization is critical to this problem. The very words *vitality* and *violence* exhibit the two faces of force (the Latin root being *vis*, force).

The dictionary definition of vitality is "the principle of life; animation, vigor, liveliness." The dictionary (Webster's Unabridged) definition of violence is "strength or energy actively displayed or exerted, esp. when destructive; vehement or forcible action; force; impetuosity; highly excited or animated force or energy."

"Esp. when destructive." Violence is the life force turned in a negative and destructive direction; vitality is the life force channeled into constructive and creative forms.

About halfway between World War I and World War II, Sigmund Freud and Albert Einstein, at the instigation of the League of Nations, undertook to write letters to one another about the relationship of vitality to violence (published as a monograph, *Why War?*, 1932). Freud as usual was not very optimistic, but he managed to find some consolation in the fact that at least both he and Einstein were pacifists, and he argued indeed that most men whose energies are expressed in intellectual creation are pacifists for what he called "organic reasons." By this he meant that as intellectual creativity increases, so does a feeling of responsibility for the sacredness of human life.

In brief, the very act of being creative serves to strengthen one's motives to preserve the results of man's constructive energies. A creative person respects the creative spark in other individual men, and in *all* men. This is one of the reasons why education for creativity is so important. Creativity is energy being put to work in a constructive fashion. Energy from human sources is greatly on the increase in the world, and the question before us is how it will be used. The research activity of psychologists and educators reported in this book is modest enough considering the importance of the problem, but it does represent an attempt to bring factual information to bear on specific issues and to advance the question somewhat so that a basis for further research and action is established.

Chapter One

The Nature
of the Problem of Creativity
for the Psychologist

The problem of psychic creation is a special case of the problem of novelty in all of nature. By what process do new forms come into being? The specification of the conditions under which novelty appears in human psychical functioning is the task to which the psychology of creativity addresses itself. In doing so, it links itself to the general scientific enterprise of describing the evolution of forms in the natural world.

Such an attempt at a purely naturalistic description of creation is itself relatively new. Creation has long been thought of as a mystery and has been deemed the province of religion or, more broadly, of the supernatural. Supernaturalism includes magic as well as religion, and may be described as an attitude of mind in which the occurrence of the unfamiliar is prone to be interpreted as an interruption of the natural course of events, or as evidence of the existence of another world. The radically novel occurrence thus borders on the uncanny and properly arouses awe.

This sense of the mystery surrounding creation is close to a universal sentiment, and certainly it may be found in the breasts of even the most scientific of psychologists as they approach the phenomenon of psychic creativity. Creativity may be defined, quite simply, as the ability to bring something new into existence. The archetype of the creator is the Divine Being; Aristotle defined the principle of generation of the universe as *nous poiēti-kos,* the poetic or creative reason. But in the divine creative act something is made to exist where nothing existed before. Since human beings are not able to make something out of nothing, the human act of creation always involves a reshaping of given materials, whether physical or mental. The "something new," then, is a form made by the reconstitution of, or generation from, something old.

To step from the putative divine case to the relatively familiar human case seems at first to remove much of the mystery. It is quickly restored, however, by considering a most common human participation in the creative act: the making of a baby. New flesh is made from old, a new form that has never lived before now comes into being. But the question quickly comes, as indeed it comes to every mother and father, even if fleetingly and darkly, "What on earth had *we* to do with this?" One speaks then of "the miracle of birth," meaning really the miracle of conception and gestation as well as parturition, and the miracle of sexuality, the male and the female principles of generation. The most primitive of emotions participate in the human act of procreation, and the sense of awe and blessedness which the mother and father may feel at the birth of their child derives in part from their recognition that a cosmic process has worked through them in a way they can only dimly understand.

In view of this universal sense of the mystery of creation, we should not be surprised if the techniques of modern psychology can offer only the most modest of beginnings to scientific knowledge in the area of psychic creativity. Indeed, the whole question of mystery may be irrelevant; certainly molecular biology in its unraveling of the genetic code has not diminished the awesomeness of the process of reproduction of living forms, nor have theoretical physics and astronomy in the picture they give us of the magnitude and age and workings, both vast and tiny, of the physical universe diminished our wonder. Quite the contrary; the revelations of science might instead lead all of us, in the back of our minds if not consciously, to be, as an intimate of Franz Kafka's once described him, "constantly amazed."

Psychology cannot as yet promise such amazing revelations concerning the process of creation in the psychic sphere, and it must still follow the older branches of science at a respectful distance. Yet in recent years there has been substantial progress in this area of study, and the vast increase in psychological and educational research has not been without effect on theory as well as practice. Most of the progress can be traced to new efforts at measurement and to new substantive inquiries directed towards the delineation of personality characteristics of notably creative human beings.

As this implies, the psychology of creativity is intimately bound up with the psychology of individual differences. Both deal with the unique, yet both aim at the description of phenomena in terms of general laws. Gordon Allport has accustomed us to think of the difficulties faced by personology as a whole by contrasting the idiographic and the nomothetic approaches to description: the former describes the individual in his unrepeatable, unexampled uniqueness, while the latter describes him in terms of common traits or factors and places him relative to other human beings on hypothesized dimensions of personality.

If this distinction is improperly understood, as indeed it has commonly been in the history of psychology, it leads to much vain argumentation and a wasteful repudiation of one or the other approach to description. The fact is that this opposition is with us constantly in all our thinking and is indeed basic to the nature of perception and thought.

The problem of establishing similarity and discriminating differences is no different in psychology than in any scientific or practical discipline. Setting oneself to the problem when the process that is of special interest is the creative process presents more poignantly, however, the paradox inherent in the classificatory tendency of mind, which is attracted alike to the common and the unique as its means. Creation implies radical novelty, whether making utterly anew or out of nothing. Yet the act of recognition that an act is creative defines in relation to creation a set of principles of classification. This would be a minor professional problem for the psychology of creativity were it not that the paradox is itself central to mind, and the individual mind shows itself creative precisely as it seeks to break out of the bounds of known classifications by raising to the highest level of consciousness the fact and the facets of its constraining conditions.

The study of psychic creation thus requires an attention to both the idiographic and the nomothetic. As psychologists we are interested in understanding a living, and hence changing, form. If our special interest is in the psychology of creativity, we wish especially to understand that form, the particular human person, in terms of its capacity to generate novelty. This means understanding its history, the forces immanent in its present way of being, its conscious and unconscious intentions and motives, its intellectual and temperamental capacities, and its place in the larger stream of events, for all of these are relevant to the creative act.

To this difficult task we must bring rather modest instruments of understanding: our tests and measurements, our interview methods, and finally ourselves both as test analyzers and as intuitive observers and participants in the interview encounter.

In my own research on creativity I have used four main sorts of intensive interviews: (1) life history; (2) professional field interview, or life work in the person's chosen field, considered in relation to life as a whole; (3) philosophy of life; and (4) openness to the irrational or the nonrational in individual experience. In what follows, I shall use primarily the "life work" interview schedule developed for a study of creative writers to illustrate my attempt to do justice to both idiographic and nomothetic considerations. Here, then, is the schedule of questions used by the interviewer as a guide to discovering the relation of the subject's creative work to his personal life.

1. *Inception and development of creative tendencies.* When did you begin thinking of yourself as a writer? Before that, was there a point at which you saw yourself as different from those around you? Your peers, siblings, parents? In what ways were you different?

2. *The crisis in philosophical belief and in personal identity.* In working out the matter of who you are, what given identities did you have to sort out and choose among? What was the religion of your parents? Were they rich or poor, relative to others in the community? What were the values, interdictions, freedoms? What were the critical moments in your development into an artist? the earliest moments of commitment?

3. *The intended audience.* Of those who may actually read the work—living people who might come upon the writing—to whom do you address yourself? Do you imagine a model or typical reader? Who is the *ideal* reader of what you have written? Who could understand it best? Of what possible readers do you think when you consider the reader as *judge* of the merit of the work? (Or, what is the jury?) Can an audience of fellow artists alone be satisfying? How important is it that common folk read and understand? Has the audience *changed* over the course of the years for you?

4. *Relation of personal growth to growth as a writer.* Do you feel that your maturation as a person has been related in any close way to the maturation as a writer? Did you grow *through* your writing? Or do you feel that an advance in personal maturity usually preceded and was necessary to an advance in artistic grasp and mastery in your work? Or is there an organic unity about the growth in both spheres, such that neither is determined by the other, but both by a common force? (Did you have experiences of suddenly "taking hold" and achieving mastery of a technique you had long been struggling with? What were the circumstances in your life and work at that time?)

5. *The act of creation.* Can you describe in detail the production of a single piece of work which you feel was especially significant for you and in which the elements of the creative act as you experience it were plainly present? Things to note: the

background of excitement, specific incitements, clarity or obscurity of the original conception, labor, incubation, inspiration, clarification (revision, and so on).

6. *Retrospective awareness.* What was going on in you that at the time of the creation you were unaware of (if anything)? Do you usually consider the work "finished" when it will pass muster as complete so far as the reading public is concerned? When your work is finished, are you "finished with it"? How do you feel at the end? elated, empty, depressed, relieved? Do your dreams change in any way you have noticed when the work is done? Do dreams influence you during the course of the work?

7. *The productive flow.* Are there noticeable ebbs and flows in your work? Are you suddenly full of ideas, or suddenly barren of them? Do you have any theory as to what might cause a sudden spurt of productivity, or a long period of drought? Think of examples of such periods: what was going on in your life or your thinking about your work at that time? Do you suffer personally from not being productive? Or are you most productive when you are suffering? Is there some work that you are putting off writing? What is it and why must you delay?

The interview on the nonrational dealt with such topics as these: divinatory dreams, precognitions, telepathy, unusual coincidences, events that were especially lucky or unlucky, falling in love at first sight, experiences of oneness with the universe, experiences of desolation or horror or utter dread, black magic, the existence of real witches or wizards in the present day, personal survival of bodily death, phantasms, poltergeist, scrying, and so on.

The philosophy-of-life interview dealt with the philosophic bases of action: ideas of good and evil, personal responsibility, the locus of ethical sanctions (whether in the individual or in society), governance or nongovernance of the universe, efficacy of or resort to prayer, and so on. One fanciful question towards the conclusion of the interview might be cited: Imagine that at death, whether to your surprise or not, you find yourself before the divine bar of justice and you are told that you are to have a jury trial and can choose for yourself the members of your jury.

Any person who has ever lived is eligible. Whom would you choose?

Another question: You have been shipwrecked on a desert island, and you are able to know for certain that you can never get off it and will never again see another human being. Would it be possible for you to commit an evil act? What might it be?

The drift of these questions is fairly clear, and one can see how they would contribute to an idiographic formulation, with the usual life history interview as a base. A major goal of these interviews was to help us answer that familiar question known only too well to the assessor of intellectual abilities: Now we know what he *can* do; but, what *will* he do? The answer to that question lies in the often hidden springs of action: in motives, intentions, values, meanings; conscious and unconscious, public and private; perhaps finally in the essentially mysterious, or in the realm of feeling that escapes naming.

It is unfashionable among optimistic and confident scientists, including psychologists, to speak of the mysterious in any way which may imply that it could be more than a present ignorance which science itself will one day abate or dissolve. Oddly enough, however, the philosophers of positivism themselves have pushed us to such questions, and idealists may obtain as much comfort as skeptics do from the writings of such original geniuses of pragmatism and positivism as Peirce, Bridgman, and Wittgenstein. I myself had my introduction to philosophical problems in psychology from the distinguished student of Wittgenstein, John Wisdom, who in the master magician's own best form delighted our seminar at Cambridge with a bag of entertaining semantic tricks. One of the scenes he created for our deliberations, I remember, involved an empty house of which we were the privileged observers 24 hours a day. One night a light went on in the house, though no one had entered it. Tradesmen whom we knew then began coming and going in the daytime, and gradually we were able to infer that a family lived there, though of course we never saw them. The family, we were given to know by Doctor Wisdom, who served as scientific know-it-all for everyone, had a cat we could all see in the light of a full moon, and indeed we did see it; almost a public cat, certainly at least a semiprivate cat (for the family, whose name turned out to be Smith, could see the cat any time at all). Alas, even to the Smiths, who were to remain forever private Smiths to us privileged observers of their house, there was something that was Smith and yet completely private. One of the Smiths developed a toothache, though none of the others had ever had one. Worse yet, when told of the toothache by an older Smith, the very youngest Smith was known to our theorist to have replied, "But I have a pain everywhere, and it is so big I think I shall die." Doctor Wisdom paused at this point and let the class have the question: "How am I to know that young Smith has such a pain?"

A silence descended on the lecture room, for now the game was going a bit far. The four Indian students of logic who were expected to provide the answers to Doctor Wisdom's questions fidgeted uncomfortably. The lone English girl who usually found the Wisdom paradoxes amusing was somber now. The Americans in the class stopped taking notes. Finally a lump of a fellow who rarely said anything at all because of his bad stammer volunteered in a single unstammering sentence the only answer that can be given when the generalized human being asks how he can know about the feelings of a particular human being: "Doctor Wisdom, you must look into your heart to find if it is so."

An old reply, of course. Intuition is at any rate one way of gaining understanding of process in personality, and in the context of discovery it is of the essence. In the context of verification, however, the nomethic approach, with its capacity to give us public knowledge about uniformities in nature, is the touchstone. In practice the two ways of working usually go hand in hand. After all, the primary data of all the branches of sciences are observations by our senses, and everything is unique; but we need to deal with observations that we can get some agreement about.

In what follows, we shall offer some examples of data and interpretation of the sort that can be called idiographic, but for the most part we shall present studies in which group averages and intercorrelations of variables within selected samples of creative individuals are the focus of attention. First, however, let us consider the kinds of problems that arise when we try to devise measures of creative thinking.

Chapter Two

The Measurement of Creativity: Definitional and Psychometric Considerations

To say, as we have, that the most common human participation in the creative act is the making of a baby, is perhaps to slight psychic creativity at the expense of material creation. Perhaps we should have said that the making of thoughts is the most common instance of human participation in the creative act.

Indeed, the two processes may not be so far apart. One baby is very much like another, and through the mechanism of genetic transmission of personal characteristics a baby may seem almost a replica of one of its progenitors. Each is absolutely unique, yet not unlike all the others, present and past. But the same is true of thoughts. It has often been noted that in some sense a man's ideas are his children, and when one studies closely a particular act of psychic creation, such as the writing of a story, one can see psychological analogues to such biological generative processes as conception, gestation, parturition, and even postpartum moodiness.

And just as every baby is both unique and typical, so is almost every thought. A man may think a thought which for him is a new thought, yet it may be one of the most common thoughts in the world when all thinkers are taken into account. His act is a creative act, but the "something new" produced is something new in the population of thoughts he can claim as his own, not something new for mankind as a whole.

These considerations are relevant to the problem of the measurement of creativity, since the statistical frequency with which a given response occurs in a defined population of responses is one kind of handy measure or index of originality. We must be careful, however, to specify accurately the population of responses which is being made to serve as a base of reference. Confusion on this point leads one to ask in absolute terms whether a given individual is "creative" or not. All of us are both creatures and creators, but we vary both in our quality as a creation and in our power to create.

Great original thoughts or ideas are those which are not only new to the person who thinks them but new to almost everyone. These rare contributions are creative in perhaps a stronger sense of the term; they not only are the results of a creative act, but they themselves in turn create new conditions of human existence. The theory of relativity was such a creative act; so was the invention of the wheel. Both resulted in new forms of power, and human life was changed thereby.

Creative power of an outstanding order is marked by the voluminous production of acts which can claim a notable degree of originality, and the occasional productions of acts of radical originality. It is instructive to read in a good encyclopedia the history of the basic scientific disciplines; one soon finds the same names cropping up in field after field, for it is the nature of genius to range with fresh interest over the whole of natural phenomena and to see relations which others do not notice.

Indeed, there is reason to believe that originality is almost habitual with individuals who produce a really singular idea. What this implies is that a highly organized mode of responding to experience is a precondition for consistent creativity. And from what we know in general about the relationship between thinking and behavior, we certainly should expect that some aspects of an individual's personality will play an important role in his capacity to think and act creatively. As a measurement area, the psychology of creativity cuts across the domains of perception, ideation, temperament, and motivation.

The kinds of behavioral products we may designate as creative are of course quite various: a novel solution to a problem in mathematics; a mechanical invention; the discovery of a new chemical process; the composition of a piece of music, or a poem, or a painting; the forming of a new philosophical or religious system; an innovation in law; a fresh way of thinking about social problems; a breakthrough in ways of treating or preventing a disease—even, heaven help us, the invention of mighty new armaments or new methods of controlling the minds of others. The important defining properties of these creative products are their originality, their aptness, their validity, their adequacy in meeting a need, and a rather subtle additional property which for the time being perhaps we can call "esthetic fit" or "elegance." The emphasis is on whatever is fresh, novel, unusual, ingenious, divergent, clever, and apt.

A primary strategic consideration in devising tests of creativity derives from the practical need for tests that can be administered to groups of subjects rather than to one subject at a time, that can be mechanically scored without the intermediation of a rater, and that depend on simple enumeration which can yield frequency distributions readily susceptible of statistical analysis. Elimination of the need for a rater should lead both to greater objectivity and to replicability; raters tend to come and go, but a mechanical scoring system will stay forever.

This set of requirements, however, immediately bumps head on into the nature of the creative act, which most commonly is quite complex and, if it is to be recognized, must have an observer capable of embracing its complexities. Emerson once declared that the person closest to the thinker of an original thought is he who first recognizes its originality. Thomas Huxley is reputed to have exclaimed, upon first hearing the statement of Darwin's theory of natural selection, "Now why didn't I think of that!" Even though he had not thought of it, he recognized immediately its originality and validity. A mechanical scoring system, so far as we know, could not have done the same. (What the future may bring in the way of inference and admiring exasperation by competing machines is another matter.)

At any rate, this difficulty still applies to the evaluation of any complex symbolic production in current practice. Consider the following four examples from the writer's own experience.

1. As the concluding section of a three-hour-long examination for a course in the Department of Social Relations at Harvard University, the following question was put to the young (Harvard) men and (Radcliffe) women in the class:

> In Part I of his "Notes from Underground," Dostoevski supposes a world in which "the psychologists" shall have finally catalogued all the responses of which human beings are capable, and all the functional relationships among such responses, so that, given the history of the entire series of events in the life of a person, or a complete description of his state at a given moment, all his subsequent actions would be predictable. Dostoevski supposes such a world in order to deny the possibility of its existence, for there is always, he says, an "except"—a final, unpredictable, unclassifiable element, which will never behave according to rational formula and in the interest of calculated advantage. And so into the state of unrelieved order and prosperity that he has imagined, Dostoevski injects "a gentleman with an ignoble, or rather with a reactionary and ironical, countenance," who arises and "putting his arms akimbo, says to us all: 'I say, gentlemen, hadn't we better kick over the whole show and scatter rationalism to the winds, simply to send these logarithms to the devil, and to enable us to live once more at our own sweet foolish will?' "
>
> In the audience to whom this question is addressed there are sitting a factorially complex factor analyst and a thoroughly analyzed and simplified psychoanalyst. The factor analyst turns to the psychoanalyst and whispers, "He's just the sort of person who would say that." "Yes," replies the psychoanalyst with an air of secret knowledge, "and at just this moment too."

What is there now for the gentleman with the ignoble or perhaps reactionary and ironical countenance to say?

This final question in the examination, the rest of which was conventional in content and easily graded, was received without alarm or undue notice by most of the class, who answered it at length with varying degrees of originality. The response most difficult to evaluate, however, was the following, in its entirety, by a Harvard student:

"Nothing; but if he were a Radcliffe girl he would fill two more blue books."

One could have wished that he had simply said nothing.

2. Graduate students serving as subjects in an assessment study were asked to construct a mosaic out of one-inch-square pieces of colored cardboard, each piece solid-colored, with a dozen or so colors available. The instructions were to build the mosaic design in a defined area, rectangular in shape, the dimensions being eight inches in height and 10 inches in width. One subject, however, turned the frame around, so that the vertical dimension was 10 inches and the horizontal dimension eight inches and he then proceeded to construct a question mark in yellow on a light gray background. Another subject selected white as the only color he would use, so that in his mosaic construction there was no definition of figure by colors within the given frame.

3. In another study, a subject was presented with cards of the Rorschach Psychodiagnostic, a set of inkblots of somewhat ambiguous form, and was asked to tell what he saw in each blot. Unlike most subjects, who take the test card and look at the blot straight on, he proceeded to inspect the card edgewise and even to bend cards in the middle to produce alterations in the area he could see. He gave responses never before heard of by the examining psychologist, a veteran of several thousand Rorschach testings.

4. A subject in a study of dreaming reported no dreams with visual content: all her dreams were of voices.

In all these cases, the rater or raters were in a quandary as to how to evaluate the response. In the study of dreams, for example, the dreams of 150 subjects had been rated for originality with very high inter-rater agreement, but this particular subject's dreams were rated either quite high or quite low. The scorer for the Rorschach test was certain that his subject's responses were "originals," for the test manual defines an original response as one which occurs no more often than once in one hundred examinations; but whether to score the responses 0-plus (a "good" original) or 0-minus (an original response which does not sufficiently respect the inkblot "reality") was difficult to decide. Artists who rated a large set of colored-paper mosaics gave the "question mark" a very low rating, feeling that it was simply manneristic and that the subject had not really done the job he was asked to do; a group of architects, however, were bemused and diverted by the all-white "non-mosaic" and thought it very clever.

The point is made at such length because of its crucial importance in the evaluation of the creative act. Can one make a valid distinction between the merely eccentric and the creative? It might be comfortable to do so after the votes are in and history has gone on long enough so that we think its verdict will not be reversed. Even then, though, one can shudder at the possibility of worlds unrevealed because the eccentricity was not met by circumstances conducive to its flowering. It is easy enough to say, as Goethe has, "The true thing is the fruitful thing," but the person who thinks oddly is often at the mercy of common opinion and perception, which are notoriously unmerciful. When he protects himself by withdrawal, what he might have generated may be lost. And if he takes another course and flies the flag of his individuality, being openly and consciously eccentric in externals, he may have to pay the price in wasted energy, public censure or ridicule, and perhaps actually loss of his pristine innocence of perception. Something of this sort may have been expressed in the concluding lines of J. P. Donleavy's novel, *The Ginger Man:*

God's mercy
on the wild
Ginger Man

The "Ginger Man" was a singular fellow, singular in perception, in innocence, and in vulnerability. You have to be lucky in finding people to care for you if you are to survive long in that condition. The creative person in a sense does something for all of us simply by being, and perhaps we help ourselves when we help such persons in the process of their own creative unfolding. It is one of the signs of the times in the United States that a social consciousness that this is so has been growing. The times need creativity, and we need to recognize it and nourish it when it comes along in the new generation (or in ourselves, for that matter).

Chapter Three

Tests of Originality, Ingenuity, and Esthetic Judgment

If we assume that acts are original only in relation to some specified commonality, then the original must be defined relative to the usual, and the degree of originality must be specified statistically in terms of incidence of occurrence. Thus a first criterion for an original response is that it should have a certain stated uncommonness in the particular group being studied.

A second criterion that should be met if a response is to be called genuinely original—a new *form*—is that it must correspond to some extent to, or be adaptive to, reality. The intent of this requirement is to exclude uncommon responses which are merely random, or which proceed from ignorance or delusion.

A variety of simple tests of originality have been developed. An example of a measure which meets the two criteria just discussed is the originality scoring of the common test, Anagrams. In one study (Barron, 1957) the test word "generation" was administered to a sample of 100 military officers. The score for originality was a count of the number of uncommon (defined in that instance as one in a hundred) *and correct* anagram solutions to the test word. Many subjects did not hesitate to offer solutions that were incorrect, and that were usually unique. In such instances, the application of the second criterion of originality was straightforward and decisive, consisting only of looking up the given spelling in a standard unabridged dictionary. Thus such solutions as "nation," "rate," and "gene" received scores of 0 because of their commonness, and such proposed solutions as "tanion," "etar," and "nege" received scores of 0 because of their unacceptability, while such comparatively rare and correct solutions as "onager," "argentine," and "ergot" received scores of 1.

A test scored by similar standards, although not by quite so unambiguous an arbiter as the dictionary, is Unusual Uses, one of the tests of the Guilford battery. The following is a hypothetical example, not drawn from the actual Guilford test. The examinee is asked to think of uses other than the common one for such an object as a sugar cube.

One quite common set of responses might be derived from the sugar cube's adaptability to service as a building block. Perhaps a less common response might be that it could be converted into a die and used for gambling. Or it could be conceived as a water-soluble building block to be used as the base of a soap castle, and to be eroded at a given rate when placed in a pan filled with 1/16 inch of water, so that the soap castle drops into the water at a specified time—the trigger of a watery time bomb, if you will. The "building block" type of response would be considered banal and scored 1 or 2 on a five-point scale; the "sugar cubes can be dice" response is a notch or two up on the originality scale and might be scored 3, or possibly 4; the fanciful idea of a watery time-bomb trigger might be scored 5, although on further thought it might be considered too zany or nonsensical to merit such a high score. Some scorers would perhaps be inclined to score it 0. The Unusual Uses test, then, does meet some criteria of desirability quite well, but there remains an area of uncertainty in the scoring.

One way to retain the advantages of a free-response test while yet employing machine scoring is to make the response a verbal one, preferably a single word, and to offer the examinee, on a multiple-choice answer sheet, several alternative initial letters, only one of which is the initial letter of the response the examiner thinks is right. Flanagan (1963) has employed a version of this technique to advantage in his Ingenuity test, and it has been used in other tests of this sort as well. Here is an illustration provided by Flanagan:

> As part of a manufacturing process, the inside lip of a deep cup-shaped casting is machine-threaded. The company found that metal chips produced by the threading operation were difficult to remove from the bottom of the casting without scratching the sides. A design engineer was able to solve this problem by having the operation performed
>
>   A. i----p h--h
>   B. m----n c--e
>   C. f----r w--l
>   D. l----d b--k
>   E. u----e d--n
>
> The two words intended by the examiner as the correct solution to this problem are "upside down," corresponding to the letters given in choice E.

There are two shortcomings in this sort of test. One is that the respondent who is clever with words but not ingenious in thinking his way through to physical solutions may arrive at the phrase "upside down" from the gestalt in alternative E and then, having gotten the words "upside down," may recognize that they do provide a good solution to the problem. This might be a sort of use of cleverness, but not the kind of *ingenuity* the test is seeking to measure.

Another objection is that an ingenious examinee may think of a fine solution which is not represented at all among the alternatives. The truly ingenious person might thus find the test extremely exasperating. Flanagan points out this difficulty, giving as an example in the above problem the possible use of a powerful magnet. He depends on the examinee's being sufficiently test-wise, or perhaps one should say test-broken, to discard the magnet solution and try to think of other types of solutions.

An interesting application of this scoring method is provided by the Remote Associates test devised by Mednick (1962). It is a clever modification of one of the tests of the Guilford battery employing a similar scoring method, and it is of interest in this context because of the logic of development, a cross between the free-response methodology and the one-right-answer type of problem. Mednick began with the idea of constructing items from pairs of infrequently occurring response words to the Kent-Rosanoff Word Association test. The published Minnesota norms to the Kent-Rosanoff provided numerous examples of responses that occurred no more often than once in a thousand. Mednick would pair two once-in-a-thousand responses, explain to the examinee how these responses were obtained, and then ask the examinee to reconstruct or recapture the original stimulus word. Suppose (again, as a hypothetical example) that the original stimulus word was "sugar." A quite common response might be "cube"; another might be "salt," or "sweet," or "tea." If one combined the two words "cube" and "sweet" and asked examinees to guess at the original stimulus word, most persons of average intelligence would soon arrive at "sugar." But if the paired words were "money" and "softsnow," both rather derivative associates of sugar as a means of persuasion, the task would be much more difficult. Mednick began with quite difficult items selected on the basis of observed statistical frequency in the Minnesota norms (p less than 0.001), but found that the test was too hard and did not yield the sorts of distributions of scores he wanted. The present published version of the test employs the same basic idea but three, rather than two, response words are given and they occur more frequently in normal associations: the words "pot," "butterflies," and "ulcer," to the stimulus word "stomach"; or the words "brick," "out," and "boat" to the word "house."

We might give one further example of a verbal test, based on the same logic as Unusual Uses but designed to tap a different dimension—capacity for metaphor. In this test (Barron, 1958), the examinee is given a stimulus image and asked to think of another image which is somewhat equivalent to it, or a metaphor for it. The test is scored both for originality and for aptness of metaphor, with the ideas of elegance and fit as two of the criteria. To the stimulus image "empty bookcases," for example, a common response is "an empty mind," or "a desert," or "a deserted room." Applying the scoring scheme for Unusual Uses, these appropriate but common metaphorical responses would receive scores of 1. "An abandoned beehive" is a more original and more apt metaphor, since it implies that the books were once active things as well as residents of their natural chamber. Busy bees, busy books, the product of busy minds; complexity of connotation, the hallmark of poetic metaphor, is at least reached for in this response, and it would be scored 3 or 4. Another uncommon response is "the vacant eyes of an idiot"; this too is an elegant and original equivalent. An empty bookcase is a mindless space; it is not just an empty space, but a vacant one, a space that was meant to be occupied, and perhaps had earlier been occupied. The vacancy is tragic; an empty bookcase is a waste.

One or two other examples should serve to make the purpose of this test clear. To the stimulus image "sitting alone in a dark room," two common responses are "lying awake at night" and, even more banal, "a bear in a cave." Two uncommon and apt responses are "one letter in a mailbox" and "a coffin in an open grave." To the stimulus image "sound of a foghorn," a common response is "a frog's croak"; an uncommon one is "a public address system announcing disaster."

Just as in tests of intellectual aptitudes in general, there has been some tendency in the development of performance tests of creativity to depend heavily on verbal materials. Nonverbal constructions are certainly of great importance, however, and in such real-life creative activities as architecture, sculpture, painting, music, mathematics, and mechanical invention the chief aptitudes needed for creation are nonverbal. Guilford has properly emphasized this point in his development of a model for the structure of intellect, and he and his associates have gone ahead and developed a variety of nonverbal tests of creativity. Since his work is presented elsewhere in this volume, we shall draw our examples from contributions by other investigators.

The work of Hermann Rorschach (1942), a Swiss psychiatrist, deserves to be mentioned first, for it has had a most important effect on theory both in the psychology of personality as a whole and specifically in theories of perception and imagination. We have mentioned it already in discussing the problems evaluating the "fit with reality" of a perceptual response which is original in terms of uncommonness, but which must meet the additional criterion of correspondence with the physical stimulus configuration that evoked it if it is to be called an "original-plus" in the Rorschach scoring.

A description of the development of the test may be found in Rorschach's monograph, *Psychodiagnostic: A Diagnostic Test Based on Perception*. The test consists of 10 inkblots, some of which contain color while others are black and white. The blots are shown one at a time to the examinee, and he is asked to say what they remind him of. The great diversity of response one finds to these inkblots—which were chosen by Rorschach after much experimentation, so that they would provide a wide sampling of important perceptual functions—makes the test a good candidate for the discovery of originality in the examinee's responses. Unfortunately, the scoring scheme is almost as ambiguous as the blots themselves, although this has not interfered with its popularity among clinical psychologists since ambiguity at least leaves room for speculation, and if the Rorschach "pigeonholes" anyone it does so quite feebly and need not be taken too seriously or conclusively. An "original" response, then, since it does not have unambiguous denotative meaning, must be evaluated in the same way one evaluates fantasy or works of art. If the examiner himself cannot "see" the form the examinee "sees," he must try to find someone else who *can* see it. If after a reasonable effort in searching, the form still proves elusive, it is considered not to be "there." History furnishes us enough examples of misguided multitudes (10 million Frenchmen have often been wrong) to make us wary of this sort of consensual verification. The Rorschach, more than any other test we have considered, confronts us with this problem.

The Rorschach has other shortcomings as well, and an effort of my own to remedy some of these difficulties in a new inkblot test led by a roundabout way to another measure of originality in inkblot perception. The effort may be worth reviewing as an exercise in test construction.

As users of the Rorschach know, the stimulus material and the scoring scheme of the Psychodiagnostic are very complex, and the test does not lend itself well to any attempt to isolate variables and to separate out their correlational components. Although this complexity is important to the test as a vehicle for clinical observation, it contributes to certain psychometric shortcomings and unnecessary difficulties when the verification of theory is the chief concern.

One important difficulty with the scoring scheme is that the number of responses varies widely for different subjects. Productivity is itself an important variable, of course, but the present method of obtaining a measure of it tends to confound the evaluation of other measures which may be equally important. Subjects now cannot be compared in terms of absolute incidence of a given type of response, since this is partly a function of total number of responses. Furthermore, subjects cannot be compared in terms of *relative* incidence, for relative incidence of response in a given category varies in some nonlinear and as yet undetermined fashion with total number of responses. This in turn is dependent to some extent on stimulus properties of the blots; there is clearly a limitation to the number of responses which can be given in any single category and, after a certain point in the production of responses, the more limited categories begin to suffer relative to the others.

What is needed, then, is a method of keeping the number of responses more or less constant for all subjects, while yet providing considerable opportunity for the subject's response tendencies to emerge. At the same time, stimulus strength should be weighted properly in evaluating response strength; one difficulty with the Rorschach measure of, for example, M tendency, is that it is a simple count of the number of human movement percepts which are verbalized by the subject, without regard for the power of the stimulus to evoke a human movement response in the average person.

Some of the difficulties were met by following these prescriptions: (a) increase the number of blots; (b) score only one response, the first, to each blot; (c) take systematic account of the relationship between stimulus strength and response tendency by employing the conventional experimental index of this relationship, namely, the response threshold; (d) isolate the main Rorschach variables and study them one at a time before attempting to study them all together.

The rationale of these prescriptions is simple and clear. An increase in the number of blots should achieve more representativeness on the stimulus side and more total-score reliability (since reliability may be increased, up to a point, by increasing test length). Scoring of only one response to each blot makes the absolute number of responses in each scoring category comparable from subject to subject, and makes feasible the use of some sort of standard score, such as Z scores, so that the individual subject's performance may be immediately referred to that of the general population. (It might be pointed out, incidentally, that Rorschach ratios, such as $M:Sum\ C$, may be much more meaningful if they are ratios of Z scores rather than absolute scores; Z ratios would be free of the often unrecognized and cumbersome assumption underlying absolute score ratios: that the blots themselves present precisely equal opportunity for the two contrasting experience types, introversive and extratensive, to manifest themselves.) The weighting of stimulus strength in evaluating response strength is essentially a more differentiated way of scoring, comparable to the use of refined rather than crude weights in prediction; the addition of the concept of threshold makes the perceptual phenomenon more assimilable to established knowledge and methods in experimental psychology, all to the good so far as Rorschach theory is concerned. Finally, the study of variables in isolation, however unholistic it may seem, may really be the best possible foundation for the understanding of variables in interaction.

Human movement was taken as the first variable to be measured in accord with these prescriptions. The model for the construction of a measure of threshold for perception of human movement was the conventional stimulus series used to determine response thresholds in such sense modalities as the auditory, olfactory, tactile, and the like. Although stimulus strength or intensity is not determinable from physical properties of the stimulus in the case of inkblots, this is no great loss so long as relative frequencies of response can be established in large samples and with some stability. By arranging inkblots of known frequency in a regularly graduated series, with p values ranging from 0.00 to 1.00, a measure analogous to the usual perceptual stimulus series is constructed. The subject's threshold for human movement is then the ordinal position of that blot in the series at which he first gives a human movement response.

The human movement response on the Rorschach test itself is thought to be a good indicator of imagination, ability to use fantasy constructively, and "inner resources." The threshold index constructed in the manner described does not correlate with such performance measures as the Guilford Unusual Uses test, but there are systematic differences between low and high threshold examinees in the expected direction. Those who react first to M potentialities are more often described by observers who have watched them for three days in a living-in assessment situation as "intelligent" and "inventive" and possessed of wide interests. Those who are not alert to human forms in the blots are seen as "simple" and "practical"; they are described as dogmatic, rigid, inflexible in thought and action, and narrow in their interests.

The M threshold blots proved readily adaptable to the scoring scheme already described for the Guilford Unusual Uses test. By tabulating frequencies of type of response to each blot, and then assigning weights of 1 to 5 in terms of "uncommonness" and "appropriateness," the test could be scored for originality.

Again, an example may help to make clear what is taken to be an original response as opposed to a banal one. One of the blots shows an ape-like figure in a crouched position. A common response is simply "an ape," or "a baboon." The crouch is interpretable as an intermediate position between a squat and the upright, however, and if one imputes lively motion to it and sees the movement as upward, the ape can be seen as leaping up. Moreover, the humanoid face can be interpreted by a bit of charitable looseness as the face of a man. Finally, by an act that can only be called imagination, the entire inkblot can be seen, as one examinee saw it, as "Rodin's Thinker shouting 'Eureka!' " In the absence of the actual inkblot, the reader will have to take this on faith, if at all, but the response really is a divertingly apt and elegant resolution of the "problem" presented by the ambiguous blot.

The mosaic construction test has already been mentioned. Samples of original and unoriginal responses to it, as well as a reproduction of the inkblot described in the preceding paragraph, may be found in the author's *Scientific American* article "The Psychology of Imagination" (Barron, 1958). In that article, too, are presented examples of unoriginal and varying degrees of original response to still another performance test, the Franck Drawing Completion test. In that test, the examinee is presented with a few lines which are to serve as the beginning of a drawing, and he is asked to complete the drawing within a given frame. This free-response test was intended by the test's author, the late Kate Franck, to measure masculinity-femininity in figural expression, but it too, like some of the other tests mentioned, proved readily adaptable to an evaluation scheme for originality.

One other kind of test, derived in large part from the work of the Gestalt psychologists, particularly Wertheimer (1954), should be mentioned. A set of such tests was adapted by R. Crutchfield (1951) of the Institute of Personality Assessment and Research and incorporated into a series known as the Insight

Puzzles test. It included such old standbys as the size-weight illusion, pinning the tail on a hidden donkey, and the word "summer" written once in longhand and joined to its mirror image upside down below it, so that the most compelling gestalt at first glance is a corkscrew-like object. The task is then to "break the gestalt," or to see a simple figure masked in a more complex one, or to get rid of an overriding preconception; in brief, to take the necessary first step in finding a new way of seeing things.

Examples might be multiplied indefinitely, and the creation of new tests of this sort is proceeding apace. In all of the creativity testing movement there is much activity, and test batteries themselves are so much in flux that no single set of measures can be said to have captured the field.

Tests similar to those we have described for the measurement of creativity in adults have been used in studies of imagination and originality in children. As long ago as 1900 some investigators were using inkblots in studies with children as well as with adults (Dearborn, 1898). Storytelling and the composition of essays and poems have long been recognized as behaviors which may be readily appraised for quality of invention and power of perception and imagination (Andrews, 1930). The drawing-completion sort of test is also an old favorite and fluency, originality, and flexibility were seen as important factors in such productions (Burchard, 1952).

Just as the Guilford group drew extensively upon its predecessors in modifying tests for more efficient use in investigations by the factor analytic method, so too have E. Paul Torrance and his highly productive colleagues, in research with children, borrowed and adapted what they could find and invented what they could not find if they thought they needed it. Adaptation of adult tests usually consisted in substituting materials, objects, or situations more familiar to children. The Consequences test, for example, was made to include such items as "What would happen if animals and birds could speak the language of men?" and instead of a Brick Uses test a Tin Can Uses test was employed.

Many tests were made up anew by the Torrance group,

again with care to draw upon materials familiar to children. In the Ask-and-Guess test, prints from Mother Goose stories such as "Tom, the Piper's Son," "Ding Dong Bell," and "Little Boy Blue" were used; the task is to ask questions about the picture and to make guesses about what might be happening or going to happen. Toys are used in the Product Improvement test; the children are asked to think of things that would make the toy more fun to play with, and of ways they could play with the toy besides the usual way.

To test originality in making up stories, children are given intriguing titles, such as "The Flying Monkey" or "The Lion That Won't Roar," and asked to make up a story to fit the title. Another test is the Just Suppose test, similar to Consequences; the examiner might ask, for example, "Just suppose that no one ever has to go to school anymore; what would happen?"

Nonverbal tests used with children have included, in addition to inkblots and drawing completions, tasks similar to mosaic constructions. In the Shape test, the child is asked to make up a picture out of many standardized shapes of colored paper. In the Circles test, he is asked to sketch objects or pictures that have a circle as a major part.

An interesting test that may also serve as a training device is the audio-tape test of B. F. Cunnington, described by Torrance (1962). Four unusual sound effects are presented and the children are asked to think of word pictures as they listen. The instructions as the test proceeds include an injunction to "stretch your imagination *further* and *further*" as the sounds are played a second and a third time.

Needs for New Tests

At a conference on the identification of creative scientific talent, held several years ago at the University of Utah (Taylor, 1957), the present writer served as reporter for a subcommittee whose task was to suggest possible new predictors of criteria of creativity in science. The report seems to have aroused little response, but some of the ideas for tests suggested by the committee may yet prove useful. A section of the report listing several possibilities is therefore given here.

Some Suggestions for Further Test Development

Highly creative individuals sometimes get very annoyed when as subjects of study they are asked to take the sorts of tests we have been describing. This need not mean that the tests are no good; persons with high IQs often are displeased with intelligence tests, just as the best student in a class will often think ill of the course examination. Nevertheless, in this case as in the other two, we might do well to heed their objections.

The objections are chiefly on these counts: (1) the tests are too superficial and in no sense do they engage the subject's deepest being, as creative work in the real world certainly does; (2) because they measure creative ability in fragments, as indeed factor analysts take pains to do, they provide no opportunity for what we have called "the integral quality of intellect" to manifest itself; (3) related to these first two objections is the third: that short and closely timed tests do violence to the very essence of the creative process, which goes at its own pace, will not be hurried, is behaviorally silent for long periods of time, and is easily aborted if someone is always blowing a whistle on it.

Practical limitations may make it impossible for the psychologist to meet these objections in the construction of new tests, but still these points may well be kept in mind as we proceed with further measurement efforts. In some research settings it should be possible to present tests which provide an opportunity for a longer gestation period, for example. In one of our own experiments (Barron, 1963), we sought to measure originality in dreaming by placing the subject in a deep trance for which he was posthypnotically amnesic and implanting a fictitious "complex" (by having the operator narrate a set of conflictful events presumably happening to the subject) and then instructing him to have a dream about the events that night while asleep. Subjects differed widely among themselves in the way in which they represented the implanted complex in their dreams, and analysis of the manifest content of the dream left little doubt that events during the rest of the trance day found expression in the dream. In other words, the dreams were "solutions" cooked up outside conscious awareness throughout the day.

The integrative tendency so important in high-level creative work is measured to some extent in several of the tests we have described earlier, but perhaps new and better measures can be devised. The prototype of what is needed is the *W* (whole blot area) score on the Rorschach, with adequate attention to the distinction between a shallow *W* and a complex and sharply conceived *W*. A test is needed that will help us to identify the kind of person that Henry James has enjoined all of us to be: "one on whom nothing is lost." This implies an open perceptual system, sharp not fuzzy, with excellent memory, and an ability to hold many ideas in one's head at once and to keep them open to complex combinations with one another.

Perhaps tests of this sort must by their nature be dependent upon the quality of discernment in the rater or scorer. Perhaps we shall need a "recognition of originality" test with which to select our scorers. To ask for tests of this degree of identity with the creative act itself may be asking too much, however. Life itself is prodigal in generating problems that challenge us to find a creative solution; this is the point at which test and criterion meet.

In this chapter we have presented various examples of tests designed to measure aspects of creativity. The examples were chosen for their relevance to the problems posed by measurement and research in an area in which the criterion variable is complex and elusive. Measurement of creative performance in nontest situations was not discussed, although the problems there are not unlike the problems of rating products and persons in the sort of miniature job samples represented by performance tests. The latter themselves, in fact, can be used as criteria for the development of nonperformance measures of correlated attitudinal and personality traits, and some examples of these were given.

Chapter Four

Creativity and Intelligence

On the face of it, the tests we have been describing as tests of originality and ingenuity seem to call for what one usually thinks of as "intelligence." If someone asked you to pick the 10 most intelligent persons of your acquaintance and then the 10 least intelligent, surely you would be surprised if the least intelligent performed as well as the most intelligent on the tests described. And even if you were simply to pick 20 persons of your acquaintance at random and rank them on intelligence, you probably would not expect such a ranking to be uncorrelated with their scores on the creativity tests.

Yet something of this sort is what we are being asked to believe by some psychologists who have done research on the relationship between creativity and intelligence. Work at the Institute of Personality Assessment and Research is sometimes cited as supporting such a view, though it is cited erroneously, as we shall see. The topic is sufficiently important to merit our consideration of the results of some of the major studies in some detail.

The "intelligence test" on which the IPAR researchers have placed most reliance is the Concept Mastery Test, developed by Lewis M. Terman and his associates in the famous Stanford study of the highly gifted. It is designed to provide differential measurement for adults in the high IQ ranges that characterized the Stanford sample as children. It is entirely verbal in content, and it tests the respondent's resources in terms of range of information, ability to use such information in analogical reasoning, English vocabulary, and ability to perceive similarities and discriminate differences in the meaning of words.

Table 4.1 presents descriptive statistics for the Concept Mastery Test on a variety of samples of adults. Those studied at the Institute of Personality Assessment and Research are shown by the designation (IPAR).

As Table 4.1 shows quite clearly, the three groups of creative individuals studied at the Institute are of quite superior verbal abiliy. The Concept Mastery Test is considered in some

TABLE 4.1.   Concept Mastery Test, Form T

Sample	N	Mean	Sigma
1. Creative Writers (IPAR)	20	156.4	21.9
2. Creative Women Mathematicians (IPAR)	16	144.0	
3. Stanford Gifted Study	1004	136.7	33.8
4. Representative Women Mathematicians (IPAR)	28	124.5	
5. Graduate students, University of California	125	119.2	33.0
6. Research Scientists (IPAR)	45	118.2	29.4
7. Medical students, University of California	161	118.2	33.1
8. Ford Foundation fellowship applicants	83	117.9	35.1
9. Creative Architects (IPAR)	40	113.2	37.7
10. College Graduates, University of California	75	112.0	32.0
11. Public Health Education applicants, University of California	54	97.1	29.0
12. Spouses of Stanford Gifted	690	95.3	42.7
13. Electronic engineers	95	94.5	37.0
14. Undergraduates, lower division, Stanford University	97	77.6	25.7
15. Military officers	343	60.3	31.6

quarters to be a very good test of general intelligence—but in Guilford's factor analytic studies of the structure of intellect the test is construed as primarily a measure of verbal comprehension. However, scores on the Concept Mastery Test in adulthood are known to be highly correlated with Stanford-Binet IQ scores of the same individuals in childhood; if one accepts the Stanford-Binet IQ as a good measure of general intelligence, then the Concept Mastery Test would qualify as the same. While only rough IQ equivalences have been established for the Concept Mastery Test, we can accept the mean of the Stanford Gifted sample as descriptive of a group whose IQ range is from about 135 to about 180. The scores of our creative writers and creative mathematicians are therefore well up in this range; in fact, only two of the creative writers made scores below the mean of the Stanford Gifted sample. The lowest scoring group of creative individuals, architects, are in the general range represented by university medical students and graduate students as well as adult research scientists, and they are markedly superior to such groups as the spouses of the Stanford Gifted and a large group of military officers, all of them of the rank of captain and at the time of testing under consideration for promotion to field grade.

Because of security regulations governing the use of the Concept Mastery Test, it could not be administered either to a comparison group of writers or to a comparison group of architects. The only sample for which a true comparison group is available is the Creative Women Mathematician sample, and the observed differences between the "creatives" and the "representatives" among women mathematicians favors the former and is statistically significant. In view of the correlation we have already noted in the military officer sample between the Concept Mastery Test and the Originality Composite, and considering also the report of Meer and Stein (1955) of a significant positive association between measured intelligence and creativity ratings among industrial chemists, this result is not surprising. The most probable state of affairs is that a low positive relationship exists between general intelligence and creativity.

The observed correlation in the sample of creative architects, however, between Concept Mastery scores and over-all rating of creativity for the 40 highly creative architects is not significantly different from 0 (—.08). A similar value was discovered in the research scientist sample studied by Gough (1961). The extremely restricted range of creativity represented by the highly distinguished architects might be expected to produce considerable attenuation in the observed correlation, of course, but as we have seen there were a substantial number of findings of a theoretically sensible sort in that sample, and there is no reason for this particular relationship to be more attenuated than the others.

In the IPAR study of architects, to be described in Chapter 6, it did prove possible to compare the highly creative group with two other samples of architects—one selected at random from the *Directory of American Architects* and the other selected so as to match the creative group in certain characteristics, such as age, geographical location of their offices, and similarity of background in training and professional experience. The comparison was made on the Wechsler Adult Intelligence Scale, widely used in individual intelligence testing and generally considered the most valid, factorially variegated, and comprehensive of the individually administered IQ tests. The group averages proved to be virtually identical, all within one point of 130 IQ in an analysis of significant differences among the groups (MacKinnon and Hall, 1968).

The generalization suggested by these findings is *not* that intelligence is unrelated to creativity, but rather that individuals of varying degrees of creativity in professions intrinsically creative in character are of quite high measured intelligence but their degree of creativity does not covary significantly with their intelligence test scores.

Another way of putting this is to say that for certain intrinsically creative activities a specifiable minimum IQ is probably necessary in order to engage in the activity at all, but that beyond the minimum, which often is surprisingly low, creativity has little correlation with scores on IQ tests.

Two other cautions should be respected in accepting even this conclusion, however. One is that an intelligence test score shows not only what an individual *can do* but what he *is willing to do* in a testing situation, which after all is part of real life and subject to interpretation as to its philosophic or moral or simply social meaning. Some people just do not like what they take to be the meaning of intelligence tests and, if they are not in the mood to do so, they will not perform. Still others are willing to cheat in order to do better. These mixed motives on the part of test respondents generally remain unknown to the tester and contribute error variance to the distribution of scores.

Furthermore, the factor analysts may be quite right in saying that the so-called intelligence tests are disproportionately loaded with verbal comprehension, and verbal comprehension moreover that reflects a specific form of socialization. In terms of this interpretation, it is not intelligence that has little or no relationship with creativity, but *intelligence tests.*

The suspicion that in most of the standardized intelligence tests the very important domain of intellectual ability, creativity, was being neglected has existed for some time. In 1898 G. V. Dearborn published in the *American Journal of Psychology* an article titled "A Study of Imagination," in which he reported the responses of Harvard students and faculty to a series of inkblots; one of his observations was that some of his more "intellectual" subjects were least imaginative. The same sort of observation was made sporadically by a variety of experimenters in the ensuing 20 years. R. M. Simpson, in an article in the *American Journal of Psychology* (1922), several years after the development of the psychometrically sophisticated Stanford-Binet Intelligence Test, was perspicuous enough to write: "Tests . . . to ascertain either native intelligence or acquired knowledge . . .(have) no elements in them to extract from the mind of the individual his powers of creative productivity and his tendencies toward originality."

Simpson proceeded to invent a number of tests of imagination for schoolchildren, and he was followed in this effort by several other psychologists, such as McCloy and Meier (1931), Andrews (1930), and Welch (1946). Correlations averaging about .25 between IQ and imaginativeness or originality were found. By the time psychologists were called upon in World War II to select men for assignments calling for a high degree of flexibility and ingenuity, it was commonly recognized that standardized measures for such traits were missing from the selection psychologist's armamentarium.

In the years since 1950 this state of affairs has become well understood among psychologists, and it has been dramatized for professional educators and intelligent laymen by a provocative study by Getzels and Jackson, published as a book in 1962 under the title *Creativity and Intelligence*. Their actual findings, unfortunately, have been somewhat misunderstood and do not entirely support the popular interpretation that has been placed upon them. There has even been a tendency to conclude that having a high IQ is a sign of *lack of creativeness*. The strongest statement that any reported finding to date would warrant is that there is no relationship at all between certain purported measures of intelligence and measures or ratings of certain aspects of creativity. Even this statement, however, is open to criticism on statistical and other grounds, as we have seen, and more definitive studies are needed.

The Getzels-Jackson study is provocative in part because that academic underdog, the student with the low IQ, seems to run off with the prize in the end, as if in reply to the pigeonholers who had given him a label based on their own notions of neat problemsolving. The most quotable portions of the study have been TAT stories told by the students who, in the nomenclature of the research, are "high creatives" *as opposed to* "high IQs." Here are a few of the stories from a "high creativity" child as opposed to a "high IQ" child. (Getzels and Jackson, 1962, p.107.)

High IQ

This is a story of counterfeiters. The man with the hat is the printer. The other man is the big boss. They are in danger of being captured by the police. They want to get out of the house. The police will arrive too late. The man and the evidence will be gone.

High Creativity

The man in the foreground is the leader of a counterfeiting ring. They have abducted the older man in the background. The older man is an excellent artist. They have kidnapped him so that they can force him to engrave the plates. He is very reluctant but they threaten to harm his wife and children so he gives in. But he draws George Washington cross-eyed and the counterfeiters are captured and he is released.

High IQ

There's ambitious Bob, down at the office at 6:30 in the morning. Every morning it's the same. He's trying to show his boss how energetic he is. Now, thinks Bob, maybe the boss will give me a raise for all my extra work. The trouble is that Bob has been doing this for the last three years, and the boss still hasn't given him a raise. He'll come in at 9:00, not even noticing that Bob has been there so long, and poor Bob won't get his raise.

High Creativity

This man has just broken into the office of a new cereal company. He is a private eye employed by a competitor firm to find out the formula that makes the cereal bend, sag, and sway. After a thorough search of the office he comes upon what he thinks is the current formula. He is now copying it. It turns out that it is the wrong formula and the competitor's factory blows up. Poetic justice!

These and a few other examples of contrasting qualities of imagination in high "IQ" and "high creativity" Ss leave the casual reader with the impression that the "high IQ" child is something of a mole while the "high creativity" child is spontaneous, amusing, unconventional, and free. Findings that are given in statistical terms, employing usually the chi-square test applied to observational categories derived from inspection of the data, include the following that were reported to be statistically significant differences between the two groups:

1. Standardized achievement measures of verbal and numerical-mathematical achievement show that both experimental groups are superior to the average of the student body, and to about the same extent—this in spite of an average IQ of 150 in the "high IQ" group and 127 in the "high creativity" (high C) group. Verbal achievement particularly is correlated with the creativity measures.

2. There were no differences between the two groups in terms of achievement motive.

3. Teachers enjoy teaching the "high IQ" Ss significantly more than they do the average student, although this difference, while in the same direction, is not statistically significant for the "high Cs."

4. In terms of such values as moral character, creativity, goal-directedness, intelligence, superior school performance, wide range of interest, emotional stability, and sense of humor, the "high IQs" believe that the traits they prefer for themselves are the ones that will lead to adult success and are favored by teachers, in contrast to the opinion held by the "high Cs" that there is no relationship between the traits they prefer for themselves and the ones favorable to adult success, and a negative relationship between traits they prefer for themselves and traits regarded favorably by teachers.

5. In the use of imagination for the creation of fantasy, "high Cs" show significantly more stimulus-free themes, unexpected endings, humor, incongruities, and playfulness, and a marked tendency toward more violence.

6. In terms of career aspirations, the "high Cs" see more occupational possibilities as open to them, as well as many more unconventional ones: adventurer, inventor, or writer, for example, as opposed to lawyer, doctor, or professor.

Getzels and Jackson attempted also to discover variables in family background that would differentiate the two groups. The findings here were sparse. The number of parents (either father or mother) who had graduated from college did not differentiate the groups, but more mothers of "high IQ" Ss had had some graduate training, and more fathers of "high IQ" Ss were employed in university teaching, in research, or in editing; "high C" fathers were more often in business. There was a slight tendency for the parents of "high IQ" Ss to have a greater age difference between them. "High IQ" mothers tended to notice more unfavorable things about their children and to emphasize "external" qualities as desirable in their children's friends, while "high C" mothers emphasized more "internal" qualities (such as standards of value, and so on).

On the whole, then, the findings do suggest more openness to experience, more flexibility, more unconventionality, more playfulness, more aggression, and more independence and inner-directedness in the "high creatives" than in the "high IQs," and thus they seem to fit in well with the pattern of results obtained in various other studies. The only trouble is that the Getzels-Jackson results cannot really be so neatly assimilated to other findings, simply because the labels "high IQ" and "high creative" are not quite accurate. The results must be entertained with certain important reservations, as the authors themselves point out. To be clear about these reservations we must keep in mind the methods the investigators employed in constituting the two groups on which they concentrated.

The subjects were 449 students in the sixth through twelfth grades in a private urban school. The mean IQ of the students, as determined or estimated from existing records (Stanford-Binet, Henmon-Nelson, or Wechsler-Bellevue Scale for Children), was 132. So, the average student in the school was in about the upper 1 percent of the general population to begin with, a crucial point in understanding the findings.

The creativity measure was a summation of five tests, four having considerable verbal component and all being significantly correlated with the IQ measure. The correlation between IQ and the summated creativity score is not given, but one of the creativity measures alone (Word Association) correlates .38 with IQ.

Both the IQ and the creativity score distributions were now dichotomized at the 80th percentile, and four groups thus defined: high-high (upper 20 percent on both measures); low-low (lower 80 percent on both measures); high-low (upper 20 percent on the IQ measure and lower 80 percent on the creativity measure); and low-high (lower 80 percent on the IQ measure and upper 20 percent on the creativity measure).

Such a procedure results in considerable reduction of sample size, of course; in this particular case, only 52 subjects of the original 449 qualified for study when these extreme groups were thus selected. The missing 90 percent includes the high-highs, who could be expected to be a small group (no more than 90, no fewer than none, and probably about 30, considering the correlations of IQ with the components of the creativity score). The high-highs are an extremely interesting group and their exclusion results in considerable loss of information.

This kind of decision on the part of the investigators is perfectly appropriate, however, and Getzels and Jackson made quite clear what they were doing, and why, and have in addition promised a further report on the high-highs. What is misleading are the labels: "high intelligence group," giving the impression that all the high intelligence subjects are included, whereas actually a subject of high intelligence would be excluded if he were also of high creativity; and "high creativity," giving the impression that all subjects of high creativity are included, whereas actually a subject of high creativity would be excluded if he happened also to have a high IQ. And besides this source of confusion, as we have already indicated, even a person designated as of "low intelligence" could have an IQ considerably above 132, since that represented the 50th percentile and hence 60 percent of the subjects with IQs greater than 132 were eligible for classification as "low intelligence"!

These considerations certainly limit the value of the findings the investigators report, especially since the information that might allow the reader to disentangle himself from the misleading nomenclature is not given. While we might agree that it is high time that the public become aware of the abuses to which indiscriminate use of IQ testing may lead, it should be clear that what advances the scientific question will in the long run be of more use to society. Repeated studies employing careful measurement offer the best hope for clarification of the degree of relationship between various aspects of intellectual functioning.

Torrance (1967) has summarized all the available evidence on the question of the relationship of creativity to intelligence by tabulating 178 correlation coefficients reported in the literature. This tabulation showed the median correlation to be .20. When creativity scores are grouped according to whether the test is primarily verbal or nonverbal, the median of 88 coefficients between intelligence and verbal creativity is .21, and the median of 114 coefficients of correlation between intelligence and nonverbal creativity is .06. At this writing, it seems very likely that future study will show these values to be not far off.

STUDIES OF INTELLIGENCE BY HISTORIOMETRY

So far as we know, the Institute of Personality Assessment and Research study is unique in having obtained intelligence test data on living individuals who are by Galton's standards "eminent," or perhaps even "illustrious." In fact, the only research offering comparable IQ estimates of persons of eminence is that reported by Catherine Cox in *Genetic Studies of Genius, The Early Mental Traits of 300 Geniuses* (1926). Her extremely painstaking research depended upon the reconstruction from biographical data, and by application of the method of historiometry, of the picture of early mental development of intellectually eminent or illustrious individuals who were born in the 400-year span between 1450 and 1850. The IQ estimate that she and her colleagues arrived at was then correlated with rank order of eminence in a sample of 282 cases. (Rank order of eminence is an index of position on Cattell's list of 1000 eminent historical personages.) The correlation proved to be .25, plus or minus .038. She presents carefully analyzed data showing that this is not due either to halo effect or to greater information about the early mental development of the more eminent.

These historiometrical studies are utterly fascinating in the details they present of the mental achievement of young geniuses. Fittingly enough, Terman himself tackled the begetter of this entire line of inquiry, Francis Galton, and the interested student might read the brief article in which he presents the evidence on Galton's IQ, which he estimates at 200 (see Terman, 1917). Here are some brief excerpts:

The Earliest Period of Instruction

From early childhood Galton was under the instruction of his sister Adele, herself a mere child. She taught him letters in play, and he could point to them all before he could speak. Adele had a wonderful power of teaching and gaining attention without fatiguing. She taught herself Latin and Greek that she might teach him. She never had him learn by heart, but made him read his lesson, bit by bit, eight times over, when he could say it. He could repeat much of Scott's *Marmion*, and understood it all by the time he was 5.

Francis knew his capital letters by twelve months and both his alphabets by eighteen months; . . . he could read a little book, *Cobwebs to Catch Flies*, when he was 2½ years old, and could sign his name before three years.

A letter written to his sister the day before his 5th birthday runs as follows:

> My dear Adele,
> I am 4 years old and I can read any English book. I can say all the Latin substantives and adjectives and active verbs besides 52 lines of Latin poetry. I can cast up any sum in addition and can multiply by 2, 3, 4, 5, 6, 7, 8, (9), 10, (11).
> I can also say the pence table. I read French a little and I know the clock.
>
> Francis Galton
> Febuary 15, 1827

We are told by Terman:

The only misspelling is in the date. The numbers 9 and 11 are bracketed above, because little Francis, evidently feeling that he had claimed too much, had scratched out one of these numbers with a knife and pasted some paper over the other.

By six, under the tutelage of Adele, Galton had become thoroughtly conversant with the *Iliad* and the *Odyssey*.

It seems that Adele also taught Francis a good deal about entomology, and at 6 and 7 years he was active and persistent in collecting insects and minerals . . .

Francis's interests . . . were not wholly literary, for at the age of 13 he gave us *Francis Galton's Aerostatis Project* . . . a series of drawings representing a flying machine. It was to work by large, flapping wings with a sort of revolving steam engine, and was supposed to carry five passengers, a pilot, and an engineer.

These are fascinating facts about young Francis Galton, and certainly we should not be surprised to learn that so brilliant and so favored a youngster became illustrious. But we might wonder, Whatever became of Adele . . . ? Of this, more later.

Chapter Five

A Method for the Intensive Study of Creative Persons

With considerable work already accomplished in the development of simple measures and the exploration of their interrelationships and their external correlates, the Institute staff turned to a method of study of exceptional promise but full of challenge and difficulties: the study by the living-in assessment method of highly creative individuals whose accomplishments in the arts and sciences, as well as industry and economic development, had already brought them renown.

It had long been recognized that the study of the lives and family backgrounds of distinguished individuals was the most direct psychological approach to an understanding of the genetic and environmental forces contributing to superior achievement. Francis Galton had shown the way in this, as in many other areas of the psychology of individual differences, by his forthright approach to biographical material in a hunt for evidence of hereditary predisposition. The volume in which his work was summed up, *Hereditary Genius* (1869), remains the most systematic and provocative analysis of the effect of family lineage on the appearance of high talent. In *Hereditary Genius* he relied on biographies for his raw data; he followed that work immediately with a study of 180 contemporary scientists to whom he sent questionnaires about their family backgrounds and their experiences in childhood, and the tabulations he made from their responses to the questions he had put to them were published in 1874 in his *English Men of Science: Their Nature and Nurture.*

It was to Galton that the monumental work of James McKeen Cattell, issuing as it has in *American Men of Science,* owes its inspiration; Cattell employed a combination of the questionnaire method and a criterion of eminence based not on biography but on current reputation within the community of science, a system of evaluation based on "voting" by one's peers which has resulted in the system of "starring" those scientists listed in *American Men of Science* who are judged to have attained eminence by this criterion. Cattell also developed a method for establishing relative degrees of eminence of historical personages and by it assembled a list of carefully ranked "1000 Eminent Men."

Galton's work with life histories was followed on the Continent by a rash of biographical studies of men of genius, many of them written from a psychiatric point of view and with a strong emphasis on psychopathology; these so-called "pathographies of genius" helped draw clinic and drawing room together in the consensus that "great wits are sure to madness near allied," as Dryden, following Seneca, had said. Havelock Ellis turned from such slanted interpretations of individual life histories to a more objective and statistical method based on a specific criterion of eminence (space devoted to the biographee in the *Dictionary of National Biography*), and his detailed analysis of over 900 eminent lives (*A Study of British Genius,* 1904) showed that the incidence of psychosis among them was certainly no greater than in the general population. (A very readable though not quite so systematic recent study, *Cradles of Eminence* [Goertzel and Goertzel, 1962], makes the point even more strongly; the incidence of psychosis was found to be considerably lower among the eminent, although eccentric behavior and various forms of behavioral pathology other than psychosis, including suicide, are much more common.)

These early studies thus broke new ground in establishing a method of investigation, and they lent two distinctive substantive emphases as well: (1) to the relationship between rare creative abilities and mental illness, or, more broadly, the relationship between intellectual talents and individual personality; and (2) to the relative contribution of environment, especially early environment, and heredity. These methods and these emphases came together to give form to the living-in assessment studies of highly creative contemporary authors, architects, and mathematicians in the late 1950's and early 1960's at the Institute of Personality Assessment and Research.

The Assessment Method

This method of study took its name from the "assessment centers" of the U. S. Office of Strategic Services, whose mission was to select men for irregular warfare assignments. It has been described in general terms in *Assessment of Men* (Murray *et al.*, 1963, reissue). Its application in a single, highly detailed case study is exhibited in *Creativity and Psychological Health* (Barron, 1963), in a chapter titled "An Odd Fellow."

Each "assessment" in the creativity researches brought together at least five distinguished practitioners in the professions chosen for study. More commonly, 10 such persons participated. The senior staff consisted of six or seven psychologists and usually one or two psychiatrists or analysts who conducted the life history interviews, A single "assessment" generally ran from Friday through Sunday, and took place in a large, comfortably furnished, former fraternity house located on a pleasant tree-lined street of such houses on the edge of the Berkeley campus. In the early days of the Institute the subjects and staff members slept in on Friday and Saturday nights, and of course took all their meals in the house and in general made it a comfortable place of residence for the weekend. A wine cellar and a fireplace added to the amenities, and in as many ways as possible the situation was defined not as test-taking but as a mutually open situation in which staff and subjects could get to know each other.

How the subjects recorded *their* observations, or whether they did at all, is not known (for the most part), but what *the staff* did at the end of the three days was this: each senior staff member wrote down all his impressions of each subject, then used a 300-word adjective checklist to characterize each subject as accurately and tersely as possible, and finally employed a 100-item set of sentences, each of them representing a clinical inference, to describe the subject in somewhat more technical and psychodynamically "deeper" terms. The Gough Adjective Checklist (Gough, 1960) was used for this first task, and the Block Clinical Q-sort (MacKinnon *et al.,* 1961) for the second.

These descriptions were given without knowledge of test results and were intended to represent what could be observed from the subject's actions and words during the three days. The full intuitive capacity of the staff observer was thus called into play, and eventually also was brought to bear on each case through the medium of a case conference and final case write-up, with test results and interview data taken into account as well. Finally, when all cases in a given sample had been studied, they were rated relative to one another on a set of 40 personality traits, based largely on the earlier conceptual formulations of Murray and of Gordon Allport (1937).

The method of selection of subjects is, of course, of central importance to the validity of the generalizations that may result from assessment studies. As an example of the development of criterion information upon which to base the choice of individuals to be studied, we present first the Institute's study of architects, which was carried out at the midpoint of the overall program and was modelled on its predecessors. A study of renowned writers chosen for their originality had already been completed, and studies of several other groups had been launched, all under the direction of various staff members of the Institute. Although each study differed slightly from the others, this particular investigation combined the features of all and may properly be considered a prototype.

Chapter Six

Establishment of the Criterion: Architecture as Example

There is no perfect solution to the problem of establishing a criterion of creativity in a professional activity. A high order of achievement is necessary if creativity is to become generally visible, but this in turn usually requires time for accomplishment and may involve other abilities besides creative ones. Much depends upon the nature of the profession. Brilliant mathematical discoveries have been made by persons under twenty years of age, and the purest voices of lyric poetry are notably those of the young. But to build many buildings or write many novels requires much time, and in most of the fields of empirical science a long preparation is necessary before techniques of experimentation can be mastered and the antecedent problems that provide a prologue for the creative breakthrough can be grasped. There is also the question. "Who really thought of it first?" which has marred the picture of scientific detachment that some people would like to think characterizes the history of science. And in evaluating the work of one's contemporaries there is always a nagging doubt as to what the verdict of history may be. To make things worse, on

what basis is one to choose the judges? Should they be the critics
or the creators themselves?

These vexing questions were with us throughout the research
as we set up practical methods for selecting subjects. The study of
architects has been chosen as an example because it illustrates
these difficulties quite clearly.

The first step in the definition of a sample was establishment
of a rule for deciding who should be considered highly creative in
the field of architecture. Recourse was had to the "nomination
and voting" method introduced by Cattell. Five senior architects
of the faculty of the College of Architecture at the University of
California, Berkeley, were asked individually to nominate, without consulting with one another, the 40 most creative architects in
the United States, and then to rate each of the 40 relative to all
the others. The following deliberately loose definition of creativity
in architecture was given as a working guide: "originality of
thinking and freshness of approach to architectural problems;
constructive ingenuity; ability to set aside established conventions
and procedures when appropriate; a flair for devising effective
and original fulfillments of the major demands of architecture:
the demands of technology, visual form, planning, human
awareness, and social purpose."

With the task thus set for them, the five nominators produced a total of 86 names; of these, 13 were nominated by all
five members of the panel, 9 by four members, 11 by three, 13 by
two, and exactly 40, as it happened, by single panel members. All
the modern giants of American architecture who were active at
that time were included in this listing.

The initial request for 40 names was linked somehow to a
decision on the part of the staff that 40 subjects would be studied
by the living-in assessment method, although in retrospect it
seems likely that some unanalyzed weakness for number magic
must have lain behind this decision rather than any rational basis
for choosing a right number for sampling. (We have, it seems,
almost always studied either 40 cases or 100 cases.) In any
event, 86 names were now on the invitation list, with 40 guests

desired. Subjects were now informed of their nomination, and their cooperation was sought, beginning with the most frequently nominated. Sixty-four in all were invited before the desired complement of 40 was filled.

The question naturally arises, was there any tendency for the more, or perhaps the less, creative to turn down the invitation? To check on this, the ratings of each of the 86 architects by the nominating panel were now re-examined and the 40 who had decided to take part in the research were compared with the 24 who had decided (for quite a variety of good reasons, it might be added) not to participate. The average ratings for the two groups were found to be virtually identical: in standard score terms, 50.00 (standard deviation 9.9) for the 24 not assessed, and 50.1 (standard deviation 9.5) for the 40 who did participate in the study.

To check further on this point, since it is such a crucial one in the selection of a sample, 11 editors of the major American architectural journals, *Architectural Forum, Architectural Record, Journal of the American Institute of Architects,* and *Progressive Architecture,* were asked to rank the 64 invited architects from most to least creative. These ranks too were converted to standard scores and average values for each architect determined; when the mean of the 40 assessed architects was compared now with the mean of the 24 who were invited but did not participate, the difference was slight and not statistically significant (51.9 for the 24; 48.7 for the 40). The slight difference that did exist could be accounted for by one case: that famous non-attender, Frank Lloyd Wright!

The architects who did take part in the assessment were also asked to rate one another (and to include themselves in the sample they were rating). Interestingly, their averaged evaluations of one another correlated .88 with the average evaluation of them by the 11 editors of architectural journals. This is an extremely high degree of agreement and approaches the reliability coefficient of the ratings themselves. It leaves little doubt that the criterion of creativity is a highly accurate one. With such fine discriminations even among the most select of master architects, the chances are very good of establishing a valid picture from the pattern of correlations with assessment variables.

The logic of the research design called for more than just correlations within a highly select sample, however. When the range of variation in the criterion variable has been so radically restricted, we can expect markedly lower estimates, from observations in such a selected sample, of the true degree of association between the criterion and its potential predictors than we might find if the entire population of architects were studied. So, even if no correlations were to appear between such ratings of creativity and the assessment variables, there might still be revealed certain group traits relevant to creative personality when the highly creative were compared with other architects unselected for creativity.

To put this another way, we might say that a comparison group of representative architects is essential if we are to be certain that the characteristics of highly creative architects are related to their creativity rather than to the fact of their being architects. And we might add that if the differences between highly creative and indifferently creative architects are similar to the correlations we find within the highly creative sample, we have strong additional grounds for believing that such differences are related to creativity.

Accordingly, another sample of architects was drawn by locating in the *Directory of Architects* 41 architects who were not numbered among the 86 earlier nominees but who were identical with them in age and in geographic location of practice. Then a further group of 43 was drawn for additional comparative purposes by adding the requirement that they should have at least 2 years of work experience and association with one of the nominated creative architects.

Thus three samples were drawn: (1) representative architects who were entirely unselected for creativity; (2) highly creative and renowned architects; and (3) architects undistinguished for creativity who nevertheless had shared space and time closely with a creative architect, and who in some sense might be thought of as "near misses."

MacKinnon and Hall, having employed both the nomination and voting technique as well as ratings, and having sampled finely to achieve interesting comparison groups, now added the further step of establishing an index of eminence by measurement of the amount of printer's ink of which the individual had been found worthy. Taking references in the *Architectural Index* as their criterion, they computed: (a) a weighted index of the number of articles by or about each architect and his work in the years 1950–1958; and (b) a weighted index of the number of pages devoted to the architect and his work for that same period. A comparison of representative with creative architects shows a clear difference.

	Articles by or about each architect	*Pages*
Representative Architects	2	3
Creative Architects	97	131

Finally, in order to be absolutely sure that these groups chosen for comparison purposes were really different in creativity, all 124 architects were cast into a single list. This list was then sent to 19 professors of architecture throughout the United States, as well as to the five professors of architecture who comprised the original nominating panel. It was also sent to every architect on the list itself, and to six editors of the major architectural journals. All these individuals were asked to rate all 124 architects on a 7-point scale in terms of creativity.

The results, when all ratings were averaged appropriately, were quite clear-cut; the "creative architects" as designated above were markedly superior to the other two groups, and the comparison group was significantly (the observed difference would occur by chance less than 1 time in 1000) more creative than the group of representative architects.

Therefore a valid criterion can fairly be said to have been established. Not only is the sample of creative architects unique, since it includes a high percentage of the most distinguished architects of the United States, but even within such a distinguished group it proved possible to make fine discriminations in terms of creative ability. A criterion of this sort augurs well for the task of discovering associated patterns of temperament, motivation, and intellectual ability.

Chapter Seven

Creative Writers, Mathematicians, and Architects

In all, three groups of eminent individuals were studied by the living-in assessment method: creative writers, mathematicians, and architects. Scientists and engineers of established productivity but comparatively less renown were also assessed, and the results of that research may be found in Chapter 9. This chapter is a sampler of findings from the work with writers, mathematicians, and architects.

The study of writers, which came first in this sequence of researches, suffered from some of the vicissitudes of ground-breaking research. For psychologists to attempt to study the creative process through firsthand contact with highly creative persons in a research setting was something new. There was by no means any assurance that such individuals would consider it worth their time and effort to make the trip to Berkeley and to spend three days taking tests. Although they were to be offered an honorarium, in itself it could not compensate them for their time. The seriousness of the enterprise was vouched for by the reputation of the University of California, and also by the sponsorship of the Carnegie Corporation, as well as by the positions of responsibility held by staff members of the Institute; but to some creative writers, for whom the stuff of both literature and life was revolt against society and contempt for the "academy," these vouchsafers were but red flags before the bull. One of the creative writers who was invited because of his early importance in the "beat" literature of the preceding decade was so little impressed by the seriousness of intent on the part of the psychologists that he used the invitation to garner a commission from *The Nation* for a piece, "The Vivisection of a Poet," exposing the folly of the study (Rexroth, 1958). Testy reactions to the first letter of invitation were not uncommon, and in some cases an exchange of four or five letters occurred before the creative writer decided whether or not to participate.

Student writers taking courses in creative writing were even touchier than their elders, and university professors teaching courses in creative writing were the most sensitive of all. On one occasion the psychologist in charge of the research, seeking the help of student writers for a study preliminary to the work with writers of high reputation, was permitted to address his request to a creative writing class, but was introduced by the instructor with this remark, "So far as I am concerned I would like to see all psychologists buried with Freud and Jung in a boxcar a hundred feet deep"—evidence of an associational process so intriguing that the bemused psychologist forgot for a moment why he was there.

But it was possible to remain philosophical about such rebuffs and to get on with the task. These of course were the extreme reactions of distaste, and they were not typical even of the invited writers who did not elect to participate in the research. Actually, architects too produced a few denunciatory rejections of the whole idea of such research, although among them, as among writers, the majority recognized the possible worth of the study and were willing to put themselves out in order to make a contribution to it. MacKinnon (1962) spoke of this as follows in the 1962 Walter Van Dyke Bingham Lecture:

The response of creative persons to the invitation to reveal themselves under such trying circumstances has varied considerably. At the one extreme there have been those who replied in anger at what they perceived to be the audacity of psychologists in presuming to study so ineffable and mysterious a thing as the creative process and so sensitive a being as a creative person. At the other extreme were those who replied courtously and warmheartedly, welcoming the invitation to be studied, and manifesting an eagerness to contribute to a better understanding of the creative person and the creative process.

It seemed, indeed, that the very greatest of the writers, who were great human beings as well, found the three days of living-in assessment profoundly engaging. Most seriously they entered into the task of looking at their work in relation to their lives and their deepest self. The psychologists and psychiatrists who interviewed these writers about their work and their life had studied the work intensively beforehand, that they might know the most significant questions to ask.

In all, a total of 56 writers participated in the research, out of 101 who were invited. Of these 56 writers, 30 were writers of high reputation whose names had been secured by a similar process to that already described for the architect study. Three professors of English, themselves creative writers, and one editor of a literary review, were asked to suggest names of writers who should be invited to take part, although they were not, as the architect nominators were, asked to suggest a specific number. Their nominations did show considerable agreement among themselves, however, and a list was drawn up consisting of 48 writers who had been suggested by at least two nominators. These writers were accordingly invited, and 26 of them accepted the invitation. Of these 26, only 17 finally did come to Berkeley for the living-in assessments, because of difficulties of scheduling groups; some last minute changes resulted in filling out the groups with three writers who had been nominated by only one nominator. Later, 10 other writers were seen either individually at Berkeley or in their own homes, giving a total of 30 participants in this phase of the research.

A comparison group was chosen from California writers who were members of a writers' association; these writers did not participate in living-in assessment, however. Most of the statistical comparisons to be drawn, therefore, will be based upon test data obtained from the comparison group by mail. The writers' study itself must be considered incomplete at this point and a full report on it will not be attempted here, but it does yield enough interesting data to justify a preliminary report.

The study of mathematicians suffers from a certain lack of symmetry in the design, stemming from practical difficulties. A total of 48 male mathematicians and 44 female mathematicians participated. The men, however, did not take part in living-in assessments, but were administered the test battery individually by the project director, Richard S. Crutchfield. The 44 women were studied by the living-in assessment method under the direction of Ravenna Helson.

Of the male sample, 26 were nominated as unusually creative by a panel of fellow mathematicians, while 22 were considered competent representatives of the profession (all held the Ph.D. in mathematics from reputable universities). The female sample is believed to include virtually every productive woman mathematician in the United States and Canada. Again a nomination technique was used to obtain the list of subjects to be invited; in this case, it consisted of 52 individuals, of whom only eight declined to, or were not able to, participate. The 44 participants were later rated by mathematicians in their own research specialties throughout the United States. From these ratings and accumulated professional opinions it seemed clear that 16 of the women mathematicians stood out from the rest of the sample as the most original and important women mathematicians in this country and Canada; the data analysis therefore concentrates on observed differences between them and the other 28 in terms of performance in living-in assessment. (Incidentally, it should be noted that fully half of the creative women mathematicians, as was true also of the men, are foreign-born. Visher's [1947] study of men starred in *American Men of Science* shows that the percentage of eminent men who are foreign-born is higher in mathematics [32 percent] than in scientific fields as a whole [17 percent].)

We turn now to a sampling of the results of these studies. A comprehensive review of the results must await publication of full reports on each study separately, and some of these are not yet available. Even a thorough first-level correlational analysis based on test measures in relationship to the criterion ratings has not yet appeared in print for the entire program of research. Nevertheless, from several papers (Gough and Woodworth, 1960; Hall, 1958), as well as from a more recent chapter in a book by the present writer (Barron, 1968) and from the mimeographed proceedings of the University Extension conference at which the first public reporting of results was made by the entire institute staff (MacKinnon *et al.*, 1961), it is possible to pull together a wealth of findings that are of scientific interest even though they have not yet been cross-validated.

Let us begin with staff descriptions of highly creative individuals as contrasted with less creative or merely representative members of the same profession. The assessment of women mathematicians can readily be made to yield such data, since 16 women of unusual creative ability were assessed, together with 28 women undistinguished for creativity. The assessment staff was of course kept in ignorance of the ratings, and, besides, eminent women mathematicians, unlike eminent architects or writers, are rarely known by reputation to anyone outside the profession. None of the psychologists except the project director had any grounds for identifying a given subject as one of the nominated "creatives." Consequently, the staff adjective descriptions and *Q* sorts obtained from the assessment staff immediately upon conclusion of the three days of assessment were free of bias and preconceptions; the task was simply to give a candid and objective description of each assessee, and the assessee's standing in terms of nominations or criterion ratings was unknown. The results of the Gough Adjective Checklist analysis are presented in Table 7.1, and of the Block *Q*-sort analysis in Table 7.2,

TABLE 7.1. *Staff Adjective Descriptions of Women Mathematicians*

Creative women mathematicians	Representative women mathematicians
At .01 level	
individualistic	cheerful
original	
preoccupied	
At .05 level	
artistic	active
complicated	appreciative
courageous	considerate
emotional	conventional
imaginative	cooperative
self-centered	helpful
	obliging
	organized
	practical
	realistic
	reliable
	sympathetic

The emphasis is upon genuine unconventionality, high intellectual ability, vividness or even flamboyance of character, moodiness and preoccupation, courage, and self-centeredness. These are people who stand out, and who probably are willing to stand up and strike out if impelled to do so. Creative people have an edge to them, it would seem from these first results.

Since no comparison group was available for the living-in assessment portion of the study of writers, it is not possible to present comparable *Q*-sort data for them. However, the composite staff description does convey a picture of their personal style. The

TABLE 7.2.   *Clinical Q-sort Items Correlated with Creativity*

r with creativity rating	Q-sort item
Positive correlations:	
.64	*Thinks and associates to ideas in unusual ways; has unconventional thought processes.*
.55	*Is an interesting, arresting person.*
.51	*Tends to be rebellious and nonconforming.*
.49	*Genuinely values intellectual and cognitive matters.*
.46	*Appears to have a high degree of intellectual capacity.*
.42	*Is self-dramatizing; histrionic.*
.40	*Has fluctuating moods.*
Negative correlations:	
— .62	*Judges self and others in conventional terms like "popularity," the "correct thing to do," "social pressures," and so forth.*
— .45	*Is a genuinely dependable and responsible person.*
— .43	*Behaves in a sympathetic or considerate manner.*
— .40	*Favors conservative values in a variety of areas.*
— .40	*Is moralistic.*

items whose averaged *Q*-sort values were either 9 or 8 on a 9-point scale are given in Table 7.3.

This composite staff *Q*-sort description of writers is not altogether unique to writers, however; a somewhat similar picture emerges in the staff's description of creative architects. Of these 13 "most descriptive" sentences, 8 are also among the most descriptive for architects; the notable exceptions, pertaining to writers but not to architects, are: "is verbally fluent; can express ideas well"; "is concerned with philosophical problems"; "thinks and associates to ideas in unusual ways"; "is an interesting, arresting person"; and "appears straightforward, forthright, candid in dealings with others." These items are replaced, in the staff description of architects, by the following: "enjoys sensuous experiences (including touch, taste, smell, physical contact)"; "has

TABLE 7.3.   Composite Staff Q-sort Description of Creative Writers

---

9's

Appears to have a high degree of intellectual capacity.
Genuinely values intellectual and cognitive matters.
Values own independence and autonomy.
Is verbally fluent; can express ideas well.
Enjoys esthetic impressions; is esthetically reactive.

8's

Is productive; gets things done.
Is concerned with philosophical problems; for example, religion, values, the
    meaning of life, and so forth.
Has high aspiration level for self.
Has a wide range of interests.
Thinks and associates to ideas in unusual ways; has unconventional thought
    processes.
Is an interesting, arresting person.
Appears straightforward, forthright, candid in dealings with others.
Behaves in an ethically consistent manner; is consistent with own personal
    standards.

---

social poise and presence; appears socially at ease"; "is a genuinely dependable and responsible person"; "is critical, skeptical,
not easily impressed"; and "concerned with own adequacy as a
person, either at conscious or unconscious levels." (This latter
item, it should be added, does appear in the fifteenth place for the
writers as well, and it reflects for both groups a common finding
from both interviews and psychological test results. The evidence
is convergent from a number of sources: creative individuals are
very much concerned about their personal adequacy, and one of
their strongest motivations is to prove themselves.)

The differences between creative writers and creative architects do make good sense. Architects are businessmen as well
as artists, and they convey a sense of practicality, dependability,
and social ease that one does not find among creative writers, on
the whole. Also, architects are not notably fluent talkers, though

of course there are some striking exceptions; the architect is more likely to be sensitive to physical materials and to sense impressions than to the flow of ideas in words. Writers are dramatists or singers, architects are builders and designers, and so one finds consistent differences in their style of being creative; but the two groups are alike in being productive and in having high standards, a wide range of interests, high intellectual ability and a high valuation of the role of intellect in human affairs, a definite sense of personal independence, and an internally consistent ethical basis for action.

So much for staff description; but what do personality and intelligence tests themselves show? What basis is there for thinking that creative individuals have an unusual amount of concern for their own adequacy as persons? What is the psychometric evidence in terms of measures of psychopathology, such as tendencies towards neurosis and psychosis? And what of intelligence? Do the tests of intellectual aptitude used in the research support the notion that creative individuals as a class are of high intellectual ability? How important is measured intelligence in determining originality, and what contribution do motivational and temperamental variables distinct from intelligence make to creativity?

For at least partial answers to these questions, we turn to the results obtained from the use of objective tests. First, there are such questionnaires as the Minnesota Multiphasic Personality Inventory (MMPI) and the California Psychological Inventory (CPI), as well as the Type Indicator based on C. G. Jung's theory of psychological types, to give some idea of the differences between creative individuals and comparison groups from the same professions in terms of personality traits, both normal and abnormal. Consider first the evidence from the MMPI which yields measures on such psychiatric dimensions as Depression, Hypochondriasis, Hysteria, Psychopathic Deviation, Paranoia, Psychasthenia, and Hypomania.

The MMPI comparisons for the samples of mathematicians are among the data not yet available in published form, but we do have such information for both writers and architects. The creative groups consistently emerge as having *more* psychopathology than do the more representative members of the same profession. The *average* creative writer, in fact, is in the upper 15 percent of the general population on *all* measures of psychopathology furnished by this test! The average creative architect is less markedly deviant, but is still consistently and substantially higher than the average for the general population on these indices of psychopathological dispositions. (See MacKinnon *et al.,* 1961, for statistics in the architect sample; the relevant average scores of the two groups of writers on the MMPI are shown in Table 7.4.)

TABLE 7.4.   *Average MMPI Scores of Creative and Representative Writers*

MMPI Scale	Creative Writers	Representative Writers
L	47	45
F	62	55
K	56	54
Hypochondriasis	63	57
Depression	65	59
Hysteria	68	58
Psychopathic Deviation	65	56
Paranoia	61	57
Psychasthenia	64	55
Schizophrenia	67	56
Hypomania	61	51
Ego-strength	58	52

From these data one might be led to conclude that creative writers are, as the common man has long suspected them to be, a bit "dotty." And of course it has always been a matter of pride in self-consciously artistic and intellectual circles to be, at the least, eccentric. "Mad as a hatter" is a term of high praise when applied to a person of marked intellectual endowments. But the "divine madness" that the Greeks considered a gift of the gods and an essential ingredient in the poet was not, like psychosis, something subtracted from normality; rather, it was something added. Genuine psychosis is stifling and imprisoning; the divine madness is a liberation from "the consensus."

If this is so, then we should expect to find evidence of an enhancement of ego strength in our creative individuals, so that greater psychopathology and greater personal effectiveness would exist side by side. Psychometrically, such a pattern would be quite unusual; the Ego-strength scale of the MMPI, for example, correlates —.60 with Schizophrenia in the general population, and —.50 with such other variables as Hysteria, Hypochondriasis, and Psychopathic Deviation.

Nevertheless, just such an unusual pattern is found, not only in relation to ego strength but in relation to the scales of the California Psychological Inventory, most of which are themselves aspects of ego strength and negatively related to the psychopathological dimensions measured by the MMPI. The average Ego-strength score for the nominated creatives among the writers is 58, and among the creative architects it is 61. In brief, they are almost as superior to the general population in ego strength as they are deviant on such pathological dispositions as Schizophrenia, Depression, Hysteria, and Psychopathic Deviation. This finding is reinforced by evidence from the California Psychological Inventory, as shown in Table 7.5, which also gives the mean scores of the representative professionals for comparison purposes.

These CPI profiles are indicative of a high degree of personal effectiveness. Creative writers are outstanding in terms of flexibility, psychological-mindedness, and the ability to achieve through independent effort as opposed to achievement through conformance; they are high also in self-acceptance, social participativeness, and capacity for gaining high social status. Creative architects are outstanding in rather similar ways: in self-acceptance, in capacity for status, in achievement through independence, in flexibility, in social participativeness, and in personal dominance.

TABLE 7.5.

CPI scale	Creative archi-tects	Repre-sentative archi-tects	Cre-ative writers	Repre-sentative writers	Creative women mathe-maticians	Repre-sentative women mathe-maticians
Dominance	59	56	55	54	46	50
Capacity for status	60	57	60	57	52	54
Sociability	48	51	52	49	42	47
Social participation	58	53	60	57	52	52
Self-acceptance	61	56	63	54	44	51
Sense of well-being	48	54	41	48	50	50
Responsibility	51	54	52	50	55	55
Socialization	47	52	42	46	45	48
Self-control	45	53	45	52	51	53
Tolerance	50	54	53	47	56	56
Good impression	43	52	44	51	46	47
Communality	48	53	49	51	41	47
Achievement through conformance	50	56	50	54	46	54
Achievement through independence	59	58	63	60	65	64
Intellectual efficiency	51	54	54	52	54	55
Psychology-mindedness	61	57	60	59	68	65
Flexibility	59	51	60	55	69	56
Femininity	57	52	62	55	53	49

Of this unusual patterning of psychopathology and personal effectiveness we have written elsewhere (1963) as follows:

> If one is to take these tests results seriously, (creative individuals) appear to be both sicker and healthier psychologically than people in general. Or, to put it another way, they are much more troubled psychologically, but they also have far greater resources with which to deal with their troubles. This jibes rather well with their social behavior, as a matter of fact. They are clearly effective people who handle themselves with pride and distinctiveness, but the face they turn to the world is sometimes one of pain, often of protest, sometimes of distance and withdrawal; and certainly they are emotional. All of these are, of course, the intensely normal traits indicated by the peaks on their profile of diagnostic scores. . . .
>
> The CPI profiles reveal also certain consistent differences between the highly creative and less creative members of the two professions. In both writing and architecture, the more creative individuals are more self-accepting and more flexible. Yet they score lower on socialization and on self-control, report less "sense of well-being," and on a scale that was developed to measure "effort to make a good impression" they score significantly lower than the general population. This latter finding probably goes along with their lower scores on "achievement through conformance." On the independence of judgment scale described earlier, being creative in the profession is substantially correlated with greater independence; the correlation is .43 in the architect total sample, and among the writers there is a highly significant difference in that direction. The average score of the general population on the Independence of Judgment scale is 8.12; representative writers scored 11.69, and creative writers 15.69.

In terms of C. G. Jung's theory of psychological types, there are again consistent differences between the more creative and the less creative members of these two professions. Creative writers and creative architects are markedly "intuitive" as opposed to "sensation" types, and are "perceptual" rather than "judging" in their orientations; in both respects they are different both from the general population and their professional colleagues. These findings are based on the Myers-Briggs Type Indicator, a questionnaire developed from Jung's theories and following quite closely his formulation in his book *Psychological Types*. This questionnaire yields scores on Introversion-Extraversion, Feeling-Thinking, Judging-Perceiving, and Intuition vs. Sensation. Only 25 percent of the general population is classified as "intuition" types by this test, yet 100 percent of the creative architects (as opposed to 59 percent of representative architects) and 92 percent of creative writers (as opposed to 84 precent of representative writers) were so classified. In terms of preception vs. judgment, 58 percent of the creative architects are the former, compared with 17 percent of representative architects.

MacKinnon discusses these test findings as follows (1962):

Employing the language of the test, though in doing so I oversimplify both it and the theory upon which it is based, one might say that whenever a person uses his mind for any purpose, he performs either an act of perception (he becomes aware of something) or an act of judgment (he comes to a conclusion about something). And most persons tend to show a rather consistent preference for and greater pleasure in one or the other of these, preferring either to perceive or to judge, though everyone both perceives and judges.

An habitual preference for the judging attitude may lead to some prejudging and at the very least to the living of a life that is orderly, controlled, and carefully planned. A preference for the perceptive attitude results in a life that is more open to experience both from within and from without, and characterized by flexibility and spontaneity. A judging type places more emphasis upon the control and regulation of experience, while a perceptive type is inclined to be more open and receptive to all experience.

The majority of our creative writers, mathematicians, and architects are perceptive types. Only among research scientists do we find the majority to be judging types, and even in this group it is interesting to note that there is a positive correlation (.25) between a scientist's preference for perception and his rated creativity as a scientific researcher. For architects, preference for perception correlates .41 with rated creativity.

The second preference measured by the Type Indicator is for one of two types of perception: sense perception or sensation, which is a direct becoming aware of things by way of the senses versus intuitive perception or intuition, which is an indirect perception of the deeper meanings and possibilities inherent in things and situations. Again, everyone senses and intuits, but preliminary norms for the test suggest that in the United States three out of four persons show a preference for sense perception, concentrating upon immediate sensory experience and centering their attention upon existing facts. The one out of every four who shows a preference for intuitive perception, on the other hand, looks expectantly for a bridge or link between that which is given and present and that which is not yet thought of, focusing habitually upon possibilities.

One would expect creative persons not to be bound to the stimulus and the object but to be ever alert to the as-yet-not-realized. And that is precisely the way they show themselves to be on the Type Indicator. . . .

Not only outstandingly creative writers but also more representative writers are predominantly intuitive, it should be noted, and the percentage difference is not great enough to be statistically significant. This tendency of professional writers in general to be both more perceptive and more intuitive than the average person probably finds expression in the kinds of inner experiences they report in our interview dealing with "the nonrational." The interview material is difficult to condense in simple statistical terms, and we do not as yet have adequate comparative data. What results are available have been presented in the volume cited earlier (Barron, 1968). Their general tendency is to indicate much more intense sensibility in writers: more openness to feelings of awe and of oneness with the universe, as well as the counterface of these, feelings of horror, forsakenness, and desolation; a more vivid dream life, with a notably greater tendency to have dreams in color, and also to have more nightmares; more hunches of an almost precognitive sort, and greater readiness to believe in prophetic dreams; yet, at the same time, skepticism about life after death and, as might be expected, a disinclination to believe in the possibility of communication between the living and the dead.

The generic disposition in these experiences and attitudes is perhaps an openness to experience on the fringes of ordinary consciousness. Many writers have spoken of the unconscious as the source of their important ideas and insights. This goes counter to the psychoanalytic notion of the unconscious as consisting of repressed mental contents. We shall return to this question later, in discussing Lawrence Kubie's theory (Kubie, 1958) that the creative process is never aided by the unconscious but only hindered by it. Writers seem to feel more friendly to the unconscious than psychoanalysts do, but we must take a closer look at the matter when we come a bit later to consider problems in the facilitation of creative thinking.

Chapter Eight

Innovators
in Business Management
in Ireland

This study was in itself a bit of an innovation, for it brought a company of California psychologists to Ireland, a country that until only a decade ago was almost entirely innocent of any "scientific" approach to matters of the mind. Though undeterred by tales of German anthropologists who had disappeared into the Irish mist or been rescued at the last minute from the clutches of an Irish bog, the Californians did approach their role in this particular innovation a bit gingerly and with certain misgivings. Who would not, remembering the gloomy overtones of Arnold Toynbee's statement in an annex to the second volume of *The Study of History*: "The romance of ancient Ireland has at last come to an end. . . . Modern Ireland has made up her mind, in our generation, to find her level as a willing inmate in our workaday Western world"? One could wonder whether psychology might not simply hasten the end of a relative isolation from material progress that had preserved, in some parts of Ireland at least, a form of purity of spirit and imagination that modern technology somehow kills. After all, cannot one ask of innovation, the constant flood of newness that science and technology especially produce, What good is it? Would we not be as well off without "the achievement motive" and "modernity"?

This study does nothing to answer such questions, nor does it undertake to try. Massive social forces bring all the peoples of the world to confrontation with the problem of maintaining integrity in the face of the challenge to traditional simplicity that modern technological progress presents. The hope of psychologists must be that they can aid people in their development through insight and understanding of psychological needs and means. Change is unavoidable, but there are choices that perhaps can be made clearer, and consequences that can be anticipated and either welcomed or avoided according to people's needs.

There are many forces making for change in the world at large—not just in Ireland. The radical increase in scientific and technological innovation is perhaps the most important. Note the exponential rate of increase of the discovery of natural forces and the isolation of natural elements since 1850; the vast increase of man-controlled power through inventions such as the steam engine, the gasoline combustion engine, the electric generator, the nuclear reactor; increased perceptual scope through telescopes and microscopes linked to photography and to radio; development of high-speed computers and automation, made possible by the increased efficiency of electronic circuits through miniaturization and improved programming; and the enormous increase in speed and scope of communication. Correspondingly rapid increases in population and in political complexities throughout the world add to a picture of change so rapid that the future is hardly predictable for even a period of ten to fifteen years.

Innovation itself may be the very basis of cultural change, as H. G. Barnett (1953) has argued. Barnett has applied certain of the ideas of gestalt psychology and of field theory to the study of social change. He defines innovation as "reorganization of a configuration of ideas." Events are interdependent; a new idea is not a specific, unitary phenomenon, but the product of a conjunction of psychological processes, none of which alone is peculiar to the pattern that generates a novel outcome. His theory has these emphases:

1. No innovation is underived; all have antecedents.

2. When innovation takes place, there is a fusion of two or more elements never previously joined in just such a fashion, so that the result is a new, qualitatively distinct unit.

3. The fusion involves a change in the pre-existing components; they are restructured in being combined. "The essence of change lies in the restructuring of the parts so that a new pattern results, a pattern the distinctness of which cannot be characterized merely in terms of an increase or decrease of the number of its component elements."

4. Quality of the new rather than quantity of combined elements defines the worth of the fusion.

5. Social or cultural institutions are linked together psychologically through *persons*. Institutions have their true embodiment in individual minds. "Institutional explanations of change, like institutional explanations of correlations, must assume a psychological foundation in the *motivations of the people who initiate and support change*" (italics mine) (p. 15, Introduction).

6. The *person who innovates* is able to reconfigurate conventional associations known and accepted by the group because he has a different starting point and a new orientation.

This personological viewpoint is the keystone of our own orientation to the psychology of social innovation. We hold that the motives for large-scale social change are furnished by a rush of events for which no single individual is alone responsible. Nevertheless, as the history of scientific discovery, technological innovation, and creative change in social and political institution shows, individuals of unusual personal force furnish the leadership and themselves *personally become the vehicles of change*. Such leaders are individual embodiments of the motives that are stirring the social organism in the large. The study of initiation and innovation in peoples comes down in practical terms to the study of individual innovators and initiators, to the study of the single person who can persuade others to adopt his views and motivate them to follow his lead.

The person who initiates cultural change must himself *be* a new kind of person, or at least the beginning of a new kind of person. The innovator is himself an innovation. And for innovation to occur on a scale large enough to bring about cultural change, there must be set in motion other social forces affecting cultural philosophy that make it easier for innovations to be produced, to survive, and finally to be accepted. In the case of Ireland, a tremendous initial impetus came from the men who led its fight for independence, the first genuine revolt from colonial rule in the twentieth century. A certain retrogression followed, however, marked by civil war, bitter religious division, and an intransigent hatred of all things English that to an outsider sometimes seems rigid as well as rigidifying. Today, however, there are new forces in motion again, spurred in part by the possible inclusion of Ireland with England in the European Common Market. Part of this new spirit accordingly is entrepreneurial, and the importance of innovation to economic well-being is being recognized by both government and private business.

IRISH INDUSTRIAL MANAGEMENT

This research was carried out in collaboration with the Irish Management Institute and was supported financially by a grant from the Human Sciences Council of the Republic of Ireland. It employed much the same assessment method and specific procedures we have described earlier. The senior staff of the Institute of Personality Assessment and Research traveled to Ireland to conduct the psychological end of the research, and the staff of the Irish Management Institute (IMI) led discussion groups and brainstorming sessions, and also took the lead in conducting career interviews with the managers who were studied. The assessments ran from Friday through Sunday and were carried out in the IMI building, a commodious mansion with spacious grounds on the outskirts of Dublin.

A word about the Irish Management Institute itself may be in order. It can correctly be described as the focal point of the efforts of Irish industry to adapt itself to modern managerial techniques. Its importance to the Irish economy was demonstrated by the fact that Prime Minister Sean Lemass himself presided at the dedication ceremonies for the new headquarters of the Institute in 1964. IMI itself was founded in 1952, with the stated objective of raising the standard of management in Ireland. It conducts very active programs of management training for its more than 6000 members and employs advanced techniques quite on a par with the best in England and the United States. The very fact that a study of the sort described in this chapter could be carried out in Ireland attests to the authority of the Institute; without its backing, no such research would have had the ghost of a chance of being accomplished.

The term "manager" as used in Ireland may require some explanation for American readers. In a recent (1966) book published by IMI, *The Management of Irish Industry,* manager is defined as follows (p. 3):

> A manager is anyone who works full-time in a firm and who is *held responsible for* a share in the managerial work of the company, that is, in making, implementing, and evaluating decisions about the application of systems of resources to achieving goals. Those whose duties are purely supervisory are to be excluded.

There are some 7000 managers in the Republic of Ireland, the IMI report shows. About 1200 of these are in firms with more than 500 employees; some 95 percent of these firms are corporate members of the Irish Management Institute. It was from among these firms, in addition to important state corporations such as Aer Lingus, that the managers in the assessment study were drawn. In most cases the general manager (chief executive) or owner of the firm was invited to participate in the research. A total of 48 individuals, selected by the IMI staff as unquestionably among the leaders in Irish economic life, received invitations, and 37 of them did participate fully in the assessments.

These Irish economic leaders represented a wide spectrum of Irish business activity: air transport, shipping, banking, building construction, manufacturing, large-scale merchandising, food processing, cigarette, dairy, and alcoholic beverage production, and a variety of public services. Half the group had offices in Dublin, and another one-third had their business addresses within the County of Dublin, though not in the city; the remainder were from scattered counties such as Wicklow, Waterford, Galway, Kildare, Monaghan, Offaly, and Sligo. Taken as a group, they are representative, in the best sense of the term, of Irish management in the mid-1960's.

The research had three goals: (1) to arrive at an accurate group description of the *persons* who constitute top-level Irish management; (2) to distinguish among these top-level industrialists the ones who are considered to be significant innovators, and to delineate ways in which they are personally distinctive; and (3) to utilize the entire group of economic leaders as a source of ideas for the Irish economy and culture as a whole.

The first of these goals was met in a joint report authored by staff members of the two institutes (Barron and Egan, 1968). The second goal will occupy us in this chapter, and the results of the group discussions and brainstorming sessions aimed at producing possibly useful ideas for Ireland are presented in the Appendix.

In brief, we shall be concerned here with differences between the more original and the less original business managers in a group that as a whole can be characterized as definitely among top management in Ireland.

ORIGINALITY

Although the process of innovation, like the creative process, is made up of a number of ingredients besides originality, it always requires original thought and action as its basis. Familiar parts must be combined in a new way, whether to make a new form or a new function. The perception of a novel possibility, and its translation into a workable reality, requires originality.

In order to study the psychological traits related to originality in this group of Irish managers, an attempt was made to appraise the novelty of their contributions *in their own fields of enterprise.* This appraisal was made by the senior staff of the Irish Management Institute. The managers and their professional careers were well known to the staff, and the final ratings came out of a "jury," or group conference, in which all the available evidence bearing on originality was considered. Originality was defined rather simply as follows: "Creativity in thinking and in approaches to problems; constructive ingenuity; ability to set aside established conventions and procedures when appropriate in favor of new ones."

Each manager was rated from 1 to 7 on this variable, with frequencies so arranged within each numerical category that the resultant distribution of ratings followed a bell-shaped curve.

These ratings were then correlated with data from the psychological assessment, including test scores, adjective self-descriptions, and the ratings and *Q* sorts given by the staff of psychologists at the end of the assessment period. Results may be conveniently divided into these four categories: (1) test scores; (2) adjective self-descriptions; (3) *Q* sorts; and (4) psychological staff ratings.

1. Test Scores Related to Originality

The California Psychology Inventory score on "Femininity" will be discussed first. Although the managers as a group scored relatively high by American norms on that scale, it was markedly *negatively* related to Originality within the group. Furthermore, there is much supporting evidence in the self-description of the more original managers, as well as in the psychological staff description of them, that they possessed to an outstanding degree various features of masculine ascendancy and dominance.

Three tests had been included in the assessment for the

specific purpose of measuring originality of ideas. One of these was the Consequences test, which presented unusual situations and asked the respondents to think up as many consequences as they could. Another test was Unusual Uses, which called upon the respondent to think of as many alternate uses as he could for various common objects. The third test was Symbol Equivalence, which presented verbal stimulus images and asked the respondent to think of poetic metaphors or "symbolic equivalences" of the stimulus images. All responses were scored in terms of originality. The scorer was in every case kept in ignorance of the identity of the respondent.

Of these three tests, only Symbol Equivalence is significantly related to originality in real-life professional behavior. This again is somewhat unexpected since usually, or in the United States at least, one does not expect originality in business matters to be related to poetic feeling and expression. It is especially unusual when taken in conjunction with the finding on masculinity, since again one does not generally see masculinity and poetical tendency as going together.

There are still other unexpected findings, however. On the Inventory of Personal Philosophy, "Fundamentalist Belief" is found to be correlated positively with Originality. The more fundamentalist the manager is, the more original he is. Moreover, the higher he scores on "Enlightened Belief," the lower he is rated on Originality. These correlations are exactly opposite to what one finds in American samples. Fundamentalist belief in the United States, however, is usually most characteristic of various Protestant sects (Lutherans, Methodists, Presbyterians, and so on). The changing meaning of psychological test variables as the social context and dominant social philosophy changes is made manifest in these results.

Several other test correlates of Originality are of marginal significance statistically. "Hypochondriasis" and "Hysteria" as measured by the MMPI are negatively related to Originality, and so is the Socialization scale of the California Psychological Inventory. Finally, the "judging attitude" of the Myers-Briggs Type

Indicator is negatively associated with Originality. The magnitude of these correlations is shown in Table 8.1 below.

TABLE 8.1. *Test Scores Correlated with IMI Originality Ratings*

Name of variable	r with originality
CPI Femininity	— .44
Symbol Equivalences	.38
Fundamentalist Belief	.35
Enlightened Belief	— .34
Myers-Briggs "Judgmental"	— .33
MMPI Hypochondriasis	— .32
MMPI Hysteria	— .30
CPI Socialization	— .30

2. Adjective Self-Descriptions Related to Originality

All 300 items of the Gough Adjective Checklist were examined for possible relationships to the IMI Originality ratings. Each manager had filled out the checklist, checking each adjective of the 300 that he felt applied to himself.

The adjective self-descriptions *positively* related to Originality are as follows:

assertive	.52
cynical	.49
strong	.48
dominant	.48
tough	.46
robust	.44
daring	.44
hardheaded	.37
bossy	.37
forceful	.36

The adjective self-descriptions *negatively* related to Originality are as follows:

pleasant .... .48
mild .... .47
understanding .... .42
modest .... .40
sentimental .... .40
unselfish .... .40
mischievous .... .40
soft-hearted .... .36

These findings hardly require comment. The more original managers are not only daring and tough, but cynical as well; the less original are "nice guys."

3. Psychological Staff Descriptions Related to Originality

The five assessment psychologists used the Q-sort deck of 100 descriptive phrases to characterize each manager at the end of the three days of observation. These descriptions were collated statistically, so that a single composite description of each manager resulted. Each phrase was then correlated with the IMI Originality ratings.

The descriptions *positively* correlated with Originality were as follows:

Is power-oriented; values power in self and others .... .62
Expresses hostile feelings directly .... .46
Values own independence and autonomy .... .44
Behaves in a masculine style and manner .... .44
Is basically distrustful of people in general; questions
   their motivations .... .44
Has high aspiration level for self .... .45
Behaves in an assertive fashion .... .42
Characteristically pushes and tries to stretch limits;
   sees what he can get away with .... .40

The descriptions *negatively* correlated with Originality were:

Arouses nurturant feelings in others .... .53
Behaves in a sympathetic or considerate manner .... .50
Behaves in a giving way toward others .... .50

Is a genuinely dependable and responsible person .... .49
Is introspective and concerned with self as an object .... .45
Is uncomfortable with uncertainty and complexities .... .40
Is concerned with own body and the adequacy of its
  physiological functioning .... .50
Judges self and others in conventional terms like "popularity,"
  "the correct thing to do," social pressures, etc. .... .39
Has a readiness to feel guilty .... .37
Gives up and withdraws in the face of frustration and
  adversity .... .34
Feels cheated and victimized by life; self-pitying .... .34

These *Q*-sort results are remarkably consistent with the self-descriptions by the managers, and they leave little doubt that the portrait we are getting is a valid one. This assumes that the IMI ratings reflect true originality. Interestingly enough, the psychologists themselves, rating originality simply from the social behavior of the managers, are in substantial agreement with the IMI staff (see Table 8.2). A three-way linkage is established: between the IMI staff ratings, the managers' self-ratings, and the psychologists' ratings.

TABLE 8.2. *Correlation of Psychologists' Trait Ratings with IMI Ratings of Managers' Originality*

	r
Sense of personal identity: self-insight and self-acceptance; and authentic, deeply rooted, socially responsible individuality which is expressed in most significant interactions	.53
Critical judgment: good insight concerning ideas—able to see to the heart of the matter; seldom wrong in his decisions about the relative merit of an idea	.38
Sense of destiny: something of resoluteness and egotism, but over and above these a belief in the foregone certainty of the worth and validity of one's attainments and future	.63
Rigidity: inflexibility of thought and manner; stubborn, pedantic, unbending, firm	—.33
Independence: not bound by the conventions of most people; seeks independence in thought, manner, activity, and belief; sees himself as free of the petty concerns and constraints of the ordinary person	.70

Inquiringness as a habit of mind: an unending curiosity about things, about people, and about nature; an inner spur toward resolutions and discernment .... .54

Impulsivity: inadequate control of impulse; lacking in self-discipline; self-centered; quick-tempered, and explosive .... .46

Breadth of interests: broad, many-faceted interests, including things outside of business .... .44

Cognitive flexibility: the ability to restructure, to shift and to adapt, and to deal with the new, the unexpected, and the unforeseen .. .57

Social acuity: observant and perceptive; quick to respond to the subtleties and nuances of others' behavior .... .42

Ideational responsiveness: stimulated by the ideas and remarks of others; sensitive to the implications of what others say and readily follows up .... .32

Cathexis of intellectual activity: values cognitive pursuits; likes to think, analyze, and understand; seeks out intellectually stimulating situations; enjoys tasks which demand intellectual effort for solution .... .43

Masculinity: characteristically masculine in style and manner of behavior; self-sufficient; not sentimental or romantic; strong ...... .49

Intellectual competence: effective utilization of the capacity to think, to reason, to comprehend, and to know .... .40

Dominance: personal ascendance in relations with others .... .49

Originality: originality and creativity of thinking and in approaches to problems; constructive ingenuity; ability to set aside established conventions and procedures when appropriate .... .55

Personal soundness: absence of serious emotional problems; stability of mood and manner; good balance of social conformity and spontaneity .... .35

4. Psychological Staff Ratings Related to Originality

Other psychological trait ratings significantly correlated with the IMI Originality ratings add convincingly to the overall picture. The most important correlates are independence of judgment, sense of destiny, cognitive flexibility, inquiringness, sense of personal identity, dominance, masculinity, and breadth of interest.

DISCUSSION AND SUMMARY

The basic aim of this study was descriptive. Leading Irish managers, considered as a group, had been described in terms of psychological tests and assessment procedures that had been used successfully by the Institute of Personality Assessment and Research of the University of California to study creative individuals in a variety of professions (*not* including business managers or entrepreneurs). Now, the relative *originality* of each manager within the group of leading managers was appraised by the staff of the Irish Management Institute on the basis of knowledge of their real-life accomplishments, and comparisons were undertaken between outstandingly original managers and the remaining representative group of top managers in Ireland.

A fundamental difficulty of interpretation exists because no comparative data for economic leaders in other countries are available; nor are there comparative data for Irish leaders in other walks of life. Until further research projected by the Institute of Personality Assessment and Research is completed, we cannot therefore know whether the descriptive results are true of managers in general, of intelligent Irishmen in general, or of Irish managers in particular.

Nevertheless, we are in a position to make meaningful comparisons between more and less original Irish managers, even though there remain difficulties of interpretation because some of the results are not consistent with previous research in the United States in which more original members of a professional group were compared with representative members of the group.

This group of leading Irish managers, taken as a whole, is impressively stable, intelligent, and socially effective. The managers, though open to innovation, do give the impression of being rather content with their lot; as a group they would not like to be original at the expense of being controversial, as they indicated in a *Q* sort designed to elicit their impressions of "the ideal manager" (Barron and Egan, 1968). But the more original among them have much more of an edge to their personalities. They see themselves and are seen by others as daring, tough, cynical, assertive, power-oriented, and unconcerned about their "popularity" or their obedience to conventional demands. At times they create an impression verging on willfulness and acerbity, though not in petty ways; they have a strong sense of destiny, independence of judgment, and cognitive flexibility and inquiringness. There is an odd combination of masculinity and sense of the poetic in them. Their vision is of conquest, mastery, personal dominance, command.

The study must be considered as an exploratory descriptive one in the absence of comparison groups. The way lies open for other studies to round out the picture, however, and to develop useful prediction equations from the assessment battery. Another group of managers of lesser stature could be assessed, for example, and compared with this group of leaders. By use of statistical procedures, variables giving maximum separation of the groups could be identified and properly weighted in an equation. This could then be used in selection for managerial posts through a variety of businesses, and its validity determined by following up the performance of the selected managers over a long enough period to give a reliable determination of on-the-job performance.

The results could also have implications for training, since it is apparent that the less original managers need to cultivate more daring and aggressiveness. Behind these traits may lie important motivational factors. A training program should try to make a "dynamic career motivational diagnosis" based on test results, observers' impressions, and interviews; with such a "personological career analysis" in hand, training could be tailored to the individual and his needs.

Chapter Nine

Productive Scientists

The earliest scientific studies of the personal traits of productive scientists employed a developed form of the comparative biographical method, similar to the historiometric method employed by Terman and by Cox in their studies of the IQs of historical geniuses.

The essential steps in the method are these two: (1) a preliminary psychogram or set of numerical trait ratings or counts, based on a search in biographical material or historical records for evidence of certain character traits; and (2) a statistical analysis of group averages in order to establish significant differences in accord with theory.

Many of the early studies grew out of an interest in the inheritance of unusual mental abilities, and personality traits as we now think of them were not in the foreground. James McKeen Cattell's research on American men of science has already been mentioned; Brimhall extended Cattell's data analysis by analyzing family resemblances (1923). Candolle (1885) had earlier done a historiometric study of the inheritance of mental traits among scientists. Odin (1895) and Clarke (1916) applied the method to the origins of great writers, and Woods (1906) used it to study intellectual and moral traits in royalty,

All these studies were relatively unsophisticated by today's standards of personality measurement, but they abound in keen observation. Although fundamental dimensional analysis of personality began about 40 years ago, only recently have psychometrically established insights into the structure of personality found application in historiometry. A later Cattell—Raymond B., nephew of James McKeen Cattell—has given an excellent example that, because it bears upon the important topic of creativity in science and has an analogue in work by R. B. Cattell and others using psychological tests with living scientists, is of special interest.

The first step in R. B. Cattell's method was recourse to biography. He reports that his extensive reading of biographies of

TABLE 9.1. *Personality Factor Scores of Eminent Researchers*
(N = 140)

Personality dimension label at minus pole	Direction of average	Personality dimension label at plus pole
Schizothymia	− −	Cyclothymia
Low intelligence	+ +	High intelligence
Low ego strength	+	High ego strength
Low dominance	+ +	High dominance
Desurgency	−	Surgency
Low group superego	0	High group superego
Threctia	+	Parmia
Harmia	+ +	Premsia
Low protension	+	High protension
Praxernia	+	Autia
Simplicity	+	Shrewdness
Low guilt proneness	0	High guilt proneness
Conservatism	+ +	Radicalism
Low self-sufficiency	+ +	High self-sufficiency
Low self-sentiment	+	High self-sentiment
Low ergic tension	0	High ergic tension

great scientists was not intended at the time to serve the end to which he finally put it in this study: it was simply his hobby. The psychograms he eventually drew, depending on his memory of his reading, consisted of variables for whose existence there was no firm evidence during the time the reading actually occurred. His qualitative observations had found expression in an earlier paper, however, and there is a convincing degree of congruence between them and the final psychographic statement.

A summary of results of another study, this one of contemporary scientists, by Cattell and Drevdahl (1955), is shown in Table 9.1; from it the reader may acquaint himself with the psychograph Cattell employed in the historiometric study. In Table 9.1 the average psychograph of 140 eminent contemporary researchers in physics, biology, and psychology is shown in relation to a general population average, a set of data of interest in itself.

The significant results of the biographical study, stated briefly, follow. Scientists are:

1. Decidedly schizothymic as opposed to cyclothymic (especially the physical scientists, such as Lord Cavendish, Dalton, Priestley, Lavoisier, Scheele, Avogadro, and J. J. Thomson)

2. Of very high intelligence

3. Of high ego strength

4. Very dominant (in a sense of dominance that includes self-assertiveness, independence, and a refusal to be bound by convention)

5. Desurgent (the desurgency factor loads highly on introspectiveness, restraint, brooding, and solemnity of manner)

Especially worth noting here are two unusual *combinations* of variables: high schizothymia with high ego strength, a finding in accord with IPAR results on other professional groups, and high dominance with high desurgency. A rather cold, introspective, solemn or even grim, strong-willed, unconventional, and highly intelligent person; this is the picture that Cattell gives us of the distinguished scientist, although he notes some striking exceptions. Humor, when present, may take a peculiar turn. Cattell recalls with relish the story that Cavendish, when dragged to a state function and about to meet some supposedly distinguished but pompous foreign scientists, broke away and ran down the corridor, squeaking like a bat. We are left in no doubt as to where Cattell stands, for he comments: "One wishes that this salutary response to pretension could be made more often."

The measures on contemporary scientists in the Cattell and Drevdahl study do support in almost every instance the findings from biographical research, although three additional factors which Cattell did not discuss can be seen as significant: emotional sensitivity (premsia), radicalism, and self-sufficiency. The premsia factor is not entirely clear, but it is believed to be an emotional sensitivity stemming from a protective parental environment.

The IPAR study of scientists employed quite different tests, but the results are consistent in many respects, particularly in terms of the California Psychological Inventory profiles for the 45 scientists studied by Gough (1961). The notable features of the group profile are summarized by Gough as follows:

> The profile for these scientists is generally elevated, a favorable indication (for effective functioning), but patterning is also visible. The scores are above average on the first cluster of scales dealing with poise and self-assurance (Dominance, Capacity for Status, Social Presence, and Self-acceptance). Then there is something of a drop on the scales assessing . . . social conformity (Socialization, Self-control), followed by another rise on the achievement indices, particularly on Achievement via Independence. The highest point on the profile occurs on the scale for psychological-mindedness, a measure of the degree to which one is interested in and responsive to the inner needs, motives, feelings, and experiences of others.

Gough's other findings showed that the scientists were of quite high intelligence, were psychiatrically stable and of high ego strength, and were unusually independent in judgment when, in the Crutchfield conformity experiment, they were put under pressure to agree with a false group consensus. In fact, as Crutchfield's data in a series of studies show, research scientists are the most outstanding in this regard among all groups studied (Table 10.1). As might be expected, on the Allport-Vernon-Lindzey Scale of Values, they are notably low in Religious, Social, and Economic values.

Creative scientists are similar to artists in the importance they give to esthetic qualities in their theories. On the Barron-Welsh Art Scale, the more original scientist differs from the less original one in preferring the complex asymmetrical figures that artists too prefer. Gough even found that the Art Scale was the single best predictor of his criterion ratings of scientific creativity, and that it had the highest weight in the best prediction equation he could derive.

It would be a mistake, then, to oppose the scientific imagination to the poetic imagination or the artistic imagination. Nevertheless, the impulse to create in science does seem to arise in rather different sorts of persons than does the impulse to create in the arts. We may have recourse once again to the Terman data. In Volume II of *Genetic Studies of Genius* we find a classification of the 301 geniuses studied by Catherine Cox into 11 subgroups, and among them, in addition to Scientists, are such groups as Artists and Imaginative Writers (Poets, Novelists, and Dramatists). These groups were characterized in terms of personal and moral qualities (67 "good traits") as well as intellectual ones. It is interesting to see the difference between scientists and the groups of imaginative writers and artists.

Artists as a group are estimated to be of lower intelligence than scientists; one basis of estimate places the average IQ at 135, although the author estimates the true IQ to be nearer 160. They are below the average of eminent men as a whole in their "average goodness," but they are notably high in "esthetic feeling," "desire to excel," "belief in their own powers," "the degree to which they work with distant objects in view," and "originality of ideas."

Imaginative writers are judged to have an average IQ of 165, and they characteristically differ from other geniuses in certain ways. They are notably high in "imaginativeness and esthetic feeling," and in a quaintly worded variable known as "amount of work spent on pleasures." They are also higher than eminent men in general in "originality of ideas," "strength of memory," and "keenness of observation"; they are lower in "soundness of common sense" and "the degree to which action and thought are dependent on reason."

The picture of scientists is not notably different from that revealed by Gough's research, though it is less complete. The average IQ is estimated as probably greater than 170. The scientific geniuses are disproportionately high, as compared with eminent individuals from all other subgroups, in "intellectual traits," "strength or force of character," "balance," and "activity." They are disproportionately low in "excitability," "sensitiveness to criticism," and various "social" traits. Cox in conclusion describes them as "a group of youths who are the *strongest* and *most forceful* and *best balanced* in the study."

Perhaps the most intriguing and eventually most useful result of Gough's research is not the further support it lends to the findings of Cattell and Drevdahl in drawing a *general* picture of the scientist, but rather the unique contribution of a descriptive and statistical basis for discovering *styles of scientist behavior* in a modern laboratory setting. Together with Donald G. Woodworth (1960) he developed a Research Scientists' *Q*-sort Deck, consisting of 56 short assertions, each referring to a mode of approach to research. Examples are: "Indifferent to the practical implications of his own research"; "Is good at developing short cuts and approximation techniques"; "Likes to talk out his research ideas and get other people's reactions"; "Takes an esthetic view; is sensitive to matters of form and elegance in research problems."

Each of the 45 scientists was asked to sort these statements into five groups in such a manner as to give a description of his own mode of approach to research problems. This made it possible to correlate scientist with scientist and so to discover subgroups of scientists who were similar to one another but different from members of other subgroups. In other words, from the 45 x 45 matrix of correlation coefficients expressing resemblances among pairs of scientists, statistical components, eight in all, were identified by factor analysis. These are, in short, types of approach to research problems, describable in terms of the original 56 assertions in the Research Scientist *Q*-sort Deck.

The eight types were named as follows, on the basis both of *Q*-sort item content and other test correlates: the zealot, the initiator, the diagnostician, the scholar, the artificer, the esthetician, the methodologist, and the independent. Their qualities are sketched by Gough and Woodworth as follows:

THE ZEALOT. This man is dedicated to research activity, he sees himself as a driving, indefatigable researcher, with exceptional mathematical skills and a lively sense of curiosity. He is seen by others as tolerant, serious-minded, and conscientious, but as not getting along easily with others and as not being able to "fit in" readily with others.

THE INITIATOR. This man reacts quickly to research problems, and begins at once to generate ideas; he is stimulating to others and gives freely of his own time; he sees himself as relatively free of doctrinaire bias—methodological or substantive—and as a good "team" man. Observers describe him as ambitious, well-organized, industrious, a good leader, and efficient. They also characterize him as relatively free of manifest anxiety, worry, and nervousness.

THE DIAGNOSTICIAN. This man sees himself as a good evaluator, able to diagnose strong and weak points in a program quickly and accurately, and as having a knack for improvising quick solutions in research trouble spots. He does not have strong methodological preferences and biases, and tends not to be harsh or disparaging towards others' mistakes and errors. Observers see him as forceful and self-assured in manner, and as unselfish and free from self-seeking and narcissistic striving.

THE SCHOLAR.   This man is blessed with an exceptional memory, and with an eye for detail and order. However, he is not a research perfectionist nor an endless seeker for ultimates. He does not hesitate to ask help when blocked in his work, and feels that he can adapt his own thinking to that of others. He is well-informed in his field, and is not given to bluffing. Observers describe him as conscientious and thorough, and as very dependable, but as lacking confidence and decisiveness of judgment.

THE ARTIFICER.   This man gives freely of his own time, and enjoys talking shop with other researchers. He is aware of his own limitations and does not attempt what he cannot do. He sees himself as having a special facility for taking inchoate or poorly formed ideas of others and fashioning them into workable and significant programs. Observers see him as honest and direct, getting along well with others, and as usually observant and perceptive and responsive to nuances and subtleties in others' behavior.

THE ESTHETICIAN.   This man favors analytical over other modes of thinking, and prefers research problems which lend themselves to elegant and formal solutions. His interests are far-ranging, and he tends to become impatient if progress is slow or if emphasis must be put upon orderliness and systematic detail. His own view of experience is primarily an esthetic one. Observers see him as clever and spontaneous, but as undependable and immature, somewhat lacking in patience and industry and indifference about duties and obligations.

THE METHODOLOGIST.   This man is vitally interested in methodological issues, and in problems of mathematical analysis and conceptualization. He is open about his own research plans and enjoys talking about them with others. He has little competitive spirit and tends to take a tolerant view of research differences between himself and others. Observers characterize him as a considerate, charitable person, free from undue ambition; at the same time they report a certain moodiness and an occasional tendency toward complicated and difficult behavior.

THE INDEPENDENT. This man eschews "team" efforts, and dislikes and avoids administrative details connected with research work. He is not a driving, energetic research man, although he does have a lively sense of intellectual curiosity. He prefers to think in reference to physical and structural models rather than in analytical and mathematical ways. Observers describe him as active and robust in manner and hard-headed and forthright in judgment. He appears relatively free from worry and self-doubt, but inclined to behave impolitely or abruptly.

This effort to delineate types is important because it gives explicit recognition to variety within a given professional grouping, even though the sample itself, like most of those that have been studied intensively, is too small to permit reliable comparisons among the subgroups thus discerned. But the point is that there are different styles of functioning and different ways of making a contribution in science, and unless we remember this fact we are liable to be misled by the consistencies we see when the method of group averages is relied upon exclusively.

The consistencies themselves are impressive. They are especially so in view of the variety of techniques employed, which have ranged from clinical interviews and projective techniques through empirically developed biographical inventories to factor-based tests. The common core of agreement from study to study requires only slight accommodation of terminology from one theoretical viewpoint to another. If we take in combination the researches of A. Roe, C. W. Taylor, R. H. Knapp, R. B. Cattell, R. D. MacCurdy, D. C. McClelland, B. Eiduson, J. A. Chambers, and H. G. Gough, and list the traits found in one study after another, this unified picture of the productive scientist emerges:

1. High ego strength and emotional stability

2. A strong need for independence and autonomy; self-sufficiency; self-direction

3. A high degree of control of impulse

4. Superior general intelligence

5. A liking for abstract thinking and a drive towards comprehensiveness and elegance in explanation

6. High personal dominance and forcefulness of opinion, but a dislike of personally toned controversy

7. Rejection of conformity pressures in thinking (although not necessarily in social behavior)

8. A somewhat distant or detached attitude in interpersonal relations, though not without sensitivity or insight; *a preference for dealing with things or abstractions rather than with people*

9, A special interest in the kind of "wagering" which involves pitting oneself against the unknown, so long as one's own effort can be the deciding factor

10. A liking for order, method, exactness, together with an excited interest in the challenge presented by contradictions, exceptions, and apparent disorder

Taylor and Barron (1963) wrote as follows in fitting together certain research observations with the nature of the process of scientific discovery itself.

> The more highly regarded young scientists are: (1) of superior measured intelligence; (2) exceptionally independent in judgment and resistant to group-endorsed opinions; (3) marked by a strong need for order and for perceptual closure, combined with a resistance to premature closure and an interest in what may appear as disorder, contradiction, imbalance, or very complex balance whose ordering principle is not immediately apparent; (4) unusually appreciative of the intuitive and nonrational elements in their own nature; (5) distinguished by their profound commitment to the search for esthetic and philosophic meaning in all experience.
>
> How, now, do such personal characteristics bear upon the meaning of scientific creativity? Science in the abstract may be

seen as a set of sentences expressing qualitative and quantitative relationships, and the history of the growth of this set of sentences may give the impression of a steady progressive differentiation and gradual enlargement of scope. As Kuhn has argued earlier, a comparison by decades of textbooks in the natural sciences would strongly support such a view. Certainly in every science there are long stretches of increasing convergence, consensus, and filling in of gaps. Thus viewed, scientific advance appears cumulative and steady.

Such a view, however, would give only part of the picture. Scientific knowledge undergoes development as a living body in much the same way as human beings do: through alternating periods of crisis and of coalescence, diffusion and integration, revolution and consensus. The image of scientific advance as cumulative is not so apt as an image of it as "development through periodic crisis which produces genuine divergence following periods of convergence." It is precisely the point at which a strong and established consensus finds itself confronted with an unassimilable fact that the forces of revolution are set in motion. These forces, as in all revolutions, threaten the established order and turn the state, in this case the state of knowledge, in a radically new direction of development. Since the forces of the revolution must be embodied in persons, what kind of person may serve as the vehicle for the change in thinking which must come? We would argue here that a person possessing the traits just described is the one most likely to be called to the task.

Briefly, let us consider the nature of those relationships.

1. The more highly developed a body of knowledge becomes, the more intelligence and capacity for discrimination and discipline is required for its mastery. The scientist who can respond creatively to crisis must therefore be of a high order of intellectual ability and must be orderly, thorough, and disciplined in his acquisition of current knowledge.

2. As discoveries occur which cannot be assimilated to current conceptions of orderliness in nature, increasing effort must be made to understand the unordered and to find a new principle which will restore order. The person who pays close attention to what appears discordant and contradictory and who is challenged by such irregularities is therefore likely to be in the front ranks of the revolutionaries.

3. If such a person then embarks on the risky business of seeking and putting forth new theories, he must be prepared to stand his ground against outcries from the proponents of the previous

but, in his view, no longer tenable consensus. He must possess independence of judgment and hold to his own opinion in the face of a consensus which does not fit all the facts.

4. Such a creative person in science must be passionately committed to his own cosmology and must respect his private intuitions, even when they seem unreasonable to himself; he must be able to open himself to sources of information which others deny to themselves.

5. Through such persons, who are embodiments of the creative process in nature, science remains alive and open to novelty; a scientific enterprise or organized scientific activity which does not allow free play to its own creative possibilities will shortly become moribund.

Chapter Ten

Creative Women

The relationship of masculinity to femininity in the creative process presents a fundamental problem. We have noted earlier that a certain femininity of interest pattern is found in creative men, even though they are of normal masculinity. Berdyaev, in *The Meaning of the Creative Act* (1954), argues that the figure of Christ is androgynous, and that all creators must be so if they are to conceive and bear greatly and whole.

Does this help us with a certain puzzle: the extraordinary preponderance of men in the ranks of the great creators in all the arts and sciences? Of the actual Adele Galton we know virtually nothing except as she appears in her brother's childhood. Virginia Woolf has written in earnest vein of an imaginary female Shakespeare (*A Room of One's Own,* 1935) who remains unknown to the world mainly for the reason that she was born a woman and not a man and was for that reason denied the opportunities her talent needed. She also wrote with high irony of the same problem in the brilliant *Orlando* (1928), who begins as a man but ends as a woman. Surely it is true that the opportunities provided by society for creative women have been severely limited; as that situation changes (and it is changing rapidly), we may discover whether some deeper psychological (biological-spiritual) motive arising from the biological basis of sexuality may not be playing a part as well. Perhaps there are fundamental and virtually unalterable correspondences between biological functions in procreation and male and female differences in creativity in the psychic sphere.

Such a speculation does not lead to the sort of questions that psychological assessment, with its emphasis on measurement and group averages, is likely to resolve. Yet the assessment method, applied to the problem of discerning the ways in which psychically creative women differ in personality and developmental history from less creative individuals (both men and women), may lead us to new insights into the social and educational problems that women face in expressing themselves creatively.

It is to research evidence centered upon some common-sense questions of this sort that we now turn.

A STUDY OF POTENTIALLY CREATIVE YOUNG WOMEN

Actually this study began with a look backward rather than forward. At Vassar College in 1954, the Mellon Foundation, at that time under the direction of Nevitt Sanford, who was on leave from the Institute of Personality Assessment and Research, began a study of Vassar alumnae. Subjects from as far back as the class of 1904 were asked to take part, and did. Most of the work involved only a series of questionnaires by mail, but for alumnae of vintage 1929 a more intensive study by the living-in assessment method was bravely proposed. As matters worked out, some of the intended total of 50 alumnae had to be drawn from classes just before or after 1929. Mary McCarthy, Vassar '30, had not yet written *The Group,* but, as it happened, the subjects of the Mellon Foundation study could well have been characters in that novel (and perhaps some of them were).

Several members of the Institute staff journeyed to Poughkeepsie to take part in the study of what proved to be an unusually independent group of women, as Crutchfield's data showed (see Table 10.1). Among them was an unusual propor-

TABLE 10.1. Resistance to Conformity Pressures, Crutchfield Conformity Experiment

Group	Number of Ss	Average conformity in percent	Resistance or independence
Males			
1. "More original" research scientists	17	10	90
2. Research scientists (total sample)	45	14	86
3. "Less original" research scientists	17	18	82
4. Engineering Honors Society (seniors)	30	20	80
5. College sophomores, University of California	52	26	74
6. Military officers	50	33	67
Females			
1. Vassar College alumnae (classes of 1929-1930)	50	22	78
2. Mills College "creatives" (seniors)	22	23	77
3. College sophomores, University of California	80	38	62
4. Mills College "controls"	29	41	59

tion of women who were quite creative as well. But also among them were some almost tragic figures of creative potential gone sour; for some, too, a crisis involving the use to which their creative intellectual abilities were to be put still lay ahead.

These women were highly intelligent, of course, and as a group they highly valued intellect and were aware of their own capacities. But most of them were good-looking as well, and some were sweet, and no one failed to be one of the three, so, as common sense would lead us to expect, they were all marriageable. And almost all did marry, some more than once. The story of the marriage was almost always the story of the life, in a way that is conspicuously absent in the life histories of creative men; and the story of the marriage was also in large part the story of what fate befell the woman's creative potential.

The focus of research in the Vassar studies was not upon creativity, and the questions about creativity that arose from it seemed to come almost incidentally, though all the more spontaneously. They were such questions as these:

> How does she perceive herself in relation to her husband's life work and *his* creativity?
> To what extent is being a mother an *intellectually* creative enterprise, and is it seen as such?
> How much is her creative ability used outside the family? At what cost, if any?
> Is creative activity outside the marriage a rejection of husband and family? Is it seen as such by them? By her? Does it arise from unhappiness within the family, or does it stem from a desire to grow and to bear fruit in all ways possible?
> Were these considerations important in the decision to marry? Did the decision mean opting for or against her own creative potential?
> What would she wish for her daughters?
> Is she fulfilled? disappointed? still waiting? too busy to notice?

These are big questions to put to a woman of age 45, and for the most part they were not put to that group of Vassar alumnae. But these questions and questions like them could be framed as part of an inquiry that looked forward rather than backward, and so they have been, in a study carried on since 1957 at the Institute of Personality Assessment and Research under the direction of Ravenna Helson, who came to the Institute staff from a teaching career at Smith College. She chose the senior year in college, Mills College in Oakland, California in this case, as the starting point for her inquiry, and she has conducted two five-year follow-ups which bring most of her subjects past the point of marriage and one or two children and show them *in medias res* with lively options all about.

DESIGN OF THE MILLS COLLEGE STUDY

Having obtained the blessing of the Mills College administration and the freely given consent of the senior class, who decided quite democratically and with ample debate at a class meeting that they were willing to take part in the research, the Institute sought from the faculty a set of names of senior women who in the faculty member's judgment had important creative potential. All members of the senior class were candidates for inclusion in this list, and all faculty members were asked to make nominations. The procedure was repeated with another senior class 2 years later, in part as a check on the early findings and in part to increase the number of cases for the continuing study of development of these women in the years after college.

The nominations from the faculty were solicited by letter. The letter emphasized originality and creativity as the traits under study and made plain that good grades, leadership, and good character alone should not qualify a student for nomination as creative; in fact, that they should be considered irrelevant. And creative *potential* was stressed; the faculty members were asked to refrain as far as they could from injecting their own predictions as to whether the potential would be realized.

About 15 percent of the senior class in the first study received nominations. Their chosen majors in college work included art, music, dance, drama, education, writing, biology, mathematics, history and government, and psychology. Only those were finally included who received multiple nominations and who were rated on originality by the faculty significantly higher than any member of a "control" group comprised of women with the same departmental majors and comparable scholastic aptitude.

The "creatives" and the "controls" were now studied both by the living-in assessment technique and by more extensive testing of a larger sample through ordinary group-testing procedures. In the living-in assessments, as in the case of Helson's earlier study of women mathematicians, the assessment staff was kept in ignorance of whether any given subject was considered a "creative" or a "control." In all, 22 "creatives" were assessed and were compared with 113 "controls," in extensive group testing. A total of 51 Mills seniors were studied by living-in assessment, 26 members of one graduating class and 25 members of another, all of whom were rated on *degree of creativity* by the Mills faculty.

Some of the intriguing developmental questions with which the study began must be left for future reports as Dr. Helson continues her observations of the lives of these women, In one of her completed reports, however, she provides data from the living-in assessment studies of the women as college seniors which makes it quite clear that potentially creative young women are very similar indeed to creative men in the ways in which they differ from appropriately chosen comparison groups (Helson, 1967). And not only do they differ from less potentially creative women in these ways, but actually they strongly resemble creative men in the variables we have found important thus far. The results suggest that on the threshold of adult life, before career and marriage choices are made, there is little difference in the important personality traits between creative women and creative men. Let us look at these findings in brief.

First of all, on both the Originality and the Complexity Scales, the Mills "creatives" score about as high as creative writers and architects (no significant difference), but significantly higher than their control group. On the Art Scale, their average score is 35.86 compared with a mean of 30.9 for the Mills control group; their average score places them just below creative architects and slightly above creative writers. The correlations with faculty ratings of creativity in this sample is .38, although in a second sample the correlation dropped to .15 and the mean score of the "creatives" dropped to 31. A recent study by McWhinnie

(McWhinnie, 1967) suggests the possibility that the Art Scale is a better predictor of artistic abilities among males than females, and further investigation of such possible sex differences is needed.

In terms of psychopathology and personal effectiveness, these potentially creative college women showed much the same pattern as we have observed in creative architects and writers. They differ from their classmates in having significantly higher scores on an MMPI index comprising such scales as Schizophrenia, Paranoia, Hypomania, and the *F* Scale, while at the same time they are higher on Ego-Strength. They produce a clear picture of effectiveness on the California Psychological Inventory, with high scores on Achievement through Independence, Flexibility, and Psychological-mindedness. Helson comments that blind interpretations of the Rorschachs of the "creatives" abound in unfavorable comments concerning their personal stability, yet a rating of Cognitive Flexibility from the Rorschach, given without knowledge of the criterion status of the subjects, correlated .78 with Potential Creativity as rated by the Mills College faculty.

The same sort of picture emerged from interviews. One interview question was, "When was the last time you cried?" Not only had the "creatives" as a group cried more recently, they also had cried *so* recently that the interviewers were sometimes startled. Four-fifths of the "creatives" as compared with one-third of the "controls" reported having experienced overwhelming feelings of emptiness, desolation, and aloneness, Preoccupation with thoughts of death and even of suicide were common in the creative group. Perhaps these findings simply reflect greater emotional intensity in these potentially creative women, but perhaps they also tell us something of the existential reality deeply experienced by young women who sense their own potential and yet despair at the prospect before them when they move out into a world which demands that they sacrifice either their femininity or their intellectual creativity.

By obtaining the cooperation of her subjects' parents in giving descriptions both of themselves and of the childhood characteristics of their offspring, Helson was able to test various hypotheses concerning the personal history of creative young women. She found that the parents of the more creative women characteristically had intense artistic and intellectual interests, placed an especially high value on moral principles, and were effective and successful persons. Children and parents felt close to one another and, although there was some tendency for the daughters to model themselves intellectually on the father to a greater extent than among the less creative group, there was no evidence of a corresponding closer companionability emotionally. In general, the more creative young women appeared to have more intellectual inclinations as children and to have a higher level of aspiration for intellectual achievement. Helson refers to these intellectual inclinations as a preference for "complex, un-stereotyped symbolic activity," which sums up a set of highly significant differences between her more creative and less creative girls in preference for such activities as these: writing poems and stories $(p<.01)$; painting, drawing, and working with clay $(p<.01)$; creating complex imaginary situations and acting in them, reading, and putting on shows $(p<.05)$; and hiking, exploring, and horseback riding $(p<.10)$.

In terms of childhood health, there was a marked tendency for the more creative subjects to have more illness and physical disability in early childhood, but to emerge as quite vigorous and robust in late childhood and to experience relatively little stress in adolescence. This is an interesting pattern that should be checked in larger samples in which good biographical data on childhood and adolescence are available.

The pattern of high level of aspiration and interest in intellectual matters in childhood clearly continued into college for these creative young women. In each of the two senior classes studied by Helson, the more creative women had more distinguished academic records than their classmates. This academic success was accompanied by more intense personal involvement in the life of the college. The college years were also years of change for them, more so than for their classmates.

The more creative women expected to marry, as indeed did virtually all the seniors; however, many more of them planned to combine a career with marriage. Helson was able to survey one of the senior classes five years after graduation, and in that class it did appear that the women who were more creative in college persisted in creative careers and did so without notable sacrifice in terms of refusing the option of marriage or happiness within marriage. One interesting test result was that the gap between creatives and noncreatives on the Complexity of Outlook Scale continued to widen, the more creative women showing a significant increase in scores while the less creative remained the same.

This pioneering developmental study continues, and it gives promise eventually of providing a picture of the full course of life in creative women. The importance of the topic can hardly be exaggerated as we move into a period of rapid change in the fundaments of family structure and in the relationships among love, marriage, sexual satisfaction, bearing of children, and expression of creative potential in women. The once dichotomous division of the sexes in social role, dress, and possession of power to determine the course of political events has been fading fast, and it is not at all implausible to argue that the cultural process itself is becoming feminized and that the most creative society of the future will develop new social forms in which masculine and feminine expression will be merged.

Chapter Eleven

Stability and Change
in Creative Thinking Abilities

Education is the process whereby potential skills or potential ways of being are made actual through *experience* as distinguished from innate developmental patterns. It is the deliberate production of changes that are considered desirable. The limits of what education can do are set by the degree of plasticity of behavior inherent in the organism, as well as by the effectiveness of educational techniques. We shall in the following chapters consider the question of education for creative thinking abilities, first by looking at some evidence for the stability and heritability of factors in intelligence, and then by looking at some recent developments in education.

Change is one of the constants in human experience. In a fundamental sense, it is not necessary to ask whether human nature is open to change; it is always changing. The proper question should rather specify aspects of human nature and ask about *rate, degree*, and *direction* of possible change.

In the case of intelligence, the specification of so complex a set of functions presents a problem in itself. Intelligence is not unitary, as decades of research dating to Galton's germinal *Inquiries Into Human Faculty* have shown. Galton and his followers —most notably Karl Pearson, Charles Spearman, and Cyril Burt —applied measurement and mathematical analysis to the domain of intellectual functions and showed quite clearly that even if we do allow for a general factor in intelligence, the so-called *g* factor, there are many specific and group factors as well.

This sort of analysis of intellectual functions into factors relatively independent of one another has been carried to conclusion during the past twenty years chiefly through the monumental program of factor analysis carried out by J. P. Guilford and his associates. We can now discern at least 60 separate factors in intellectual behavior. What lies behind them at the structural-anatomical level or in terms of central nervous system functioning is still anyone's guess; and the thorny problem of the relative influence of heredity and environment must be approached anew for each factor separately. In terms of this view of intelligence as factorially quite complex, psychological science as yet has no answers to give to questions about rate, degree, and direction of change.

In spite of this, we are not wholly at a loss. Granting the shortcomings of the intelligence tests now in common use, some of which have a history of use for more than fifty years, we have reason to believe that they provide reliable and accurate measurement of a combination of some of the more important factors in practical intelligence, such as verbal comprehension, verbal and numerical reasoning, and various manifestations of fluency and flexibility. What they most notably fail to measure, as we have shown at length, are some of the functions important to creativity and imagination, such as originality. For the moment, however, while keeping this in mind, let us look at the evidence concerning stability and change in intelligence if we accept the definition so popular in the 1930's, "intelligence is what the intelligence tests measure."

Such tests of general intelligence as the Stanford-Binet, the Otis, the Wechsler-Bellevue, and the Kuhlman-Anderson have been administered repeatedly to the same individuals in several major longitudinal studies, such as the Harvard Growth Study, the University of Chicago Study, the California Guidance Study, and the Berkeley Growth Study. The results are consistent from study to study, though with minor variations. Typical findings are those of Bayley (1949) based on an analysis of the Berkeley Growth Study data on intelligence from age 1 to age 18. Intelligence at age 1 correlates *.41* with intelligence at age 18; by age 2 the correlation is *.55;* by age 7 it is over *.80,* and by age 11 it is *.96,* approximately the reliability of the test. These are grouped data, that is, they are averages based on several administrations at a given age level to compensate for errors of measurement arising from small differences from occasion to occasion.

The meaning of this set of findings, and similar results from other studies, is quite clear: When proper care is taken experimentally to eliminate chance variation, general intelligence is an exceptionally stable characteristic of the individual.

Cross-sectional studies of populations in relatively homogeneous environments, such as school populations in a given city from year to year, show that intelligence as expressed in terms of range of IQ, mean IQ, and variability is extremely stable. We do not have such data over very long periods of time, but history provides no contrary evidence to the claim that human intelligence has existed within the same general range of variation for ae least 2500 years—and probably very much longer. Indeed, Volume 2 of the famous Terman studies, *Genetic Studies of Genius,* contains compelling evidence based on the historiometric method as applied by Catherine Cox to the biographies of 301 geniuses who lived between 1450 and 1850 that the upper limits are quite consistent from century to century. And if we hearken back to Aristotle and other geniuses in the childhood of our modern culture, we should certainly conclude that as a species we are getting no brighter. The most plausible generalization seems to be that stability of intelligence in populations over time is as great as it is in the individual in our own generation.

This is not to say that change cannot be produced, however, either in the individual or in the species, if it becomes sufficiently important to us to effect such change. But certain hard decisions would be entailed, some of which are not likely to be taken simply because of social resistance to them and the difficulties they would present when feasible political action is the test; and still others are morally repugnant. Such decisions might involve planned change in either heredity or environments, or in both.

Galton himself has left us a legacy of information concerning possible eugenic measures that might be taken. He felt so strongly about the need to improve intelligence by rational eugenic decisions, especially in the face of the rapid mitigation by medical science and social welfare of the severe process of natural selection, that his last years were dedicated to the propagation of eugenics almost as a religious movement. Even in England, however, he could rouse no great enthusiasm, and the very earnestness of the eugenicists made them the butt of jokes. George Bernard Shaw's reply to the stage beauty who proposed to conjoin their genetic streams to produce a child with her body and his brains is well known: "But my dear, think of the consequences should he have *my* body and *your* brains."

Popular jokes aside, Galton put the matter in objective terms and stated the nature-nurture problem in a way that made it open to measurement and to specification of the relative degrees of contribution of heredity and environment. He evolved the conception that the germ plasm of the individual is not peculiar to the individual but to a genetic stream (the stirp) for which the individual organism is only a conduit. Out of this came his inference that the somatic characteristics of the next generation cannot be modified by altering the somatic characteristics of the parent generation; this can be done only by influencing the reproductive cells. From this followed immediately his statement of the nature-nurture problem. His disciple, Karl Pearson, has summarized it as follows:

We find a variety of stirps in the community; these give a definite mean character, and a definite variability about that mean; we find also definite grades of environment subject to which the species can exist. These grades of environment have again their mean character and definite variability. This variability may be due to variability of physical conditions, or in the case of man to political, social, and economic conditions. If we give equal divergences from mediocrity measured in their units of variation to the stirp and to the environment, which will produce the greater effect on the somatic characters of the offspring?

The answer in broad lines has been invariably the same, the differences in the offspring produced by a difference of stirp are immensely more important than those which can be produced by any absolute variations of environment which seem politically or socially feasible.

We should hold in abeyance for the moment this latter part of Pearson's statement, since times have changed somewhat and we need to take a fresh look at the problem of the effects that may be produced by changes in the social, economic, and intellectual environment. Yet we must admit that experience up to the present would tend to support his statement. The bases on which general intelligence are developed are clearly inherited, and in a homogeneous environment the genetic factors probably account for almost all the variation in intelligence. In identical twins reared together, for example, the twin-pair correlations range from .90 to .95, again close to the reliability of the tests. In identical twins who are reared apart, however, the correlations average about .75, reflecting differential influence from the environment. Nonidentical twins reared together are only very slightly more similar than ordinary siblings reared together, and these in turn are significantly more similar than ordinary siblings reared apart. Finally, unrelated children reared together are significantly more alike than unrelated children reared apart, although the correlation is only about .25. Still, the meaning is clear: At the extremes of relatedness, from 5 percent to 10 percent of the variation in intelligence is a function of environment; the rest is a function of heredity.

This conclusion gives special importance to recent developments in molecular biology and to technical advances in methods of contraception and of artificial insemination. Further work in the unraveling of the genetic code may very well lead to a radical revision in our estimates of the possibility of influencing the basic mechanisms of heredity. Such basic scientific advances combined with increased technological control over births may place for the first time in the hands of man the means for influencing some of his own most distinctive characteristics, including intelligence.

It is hardly necessary to draw out the implications of these developments in terms of social problems, including that of national ascendancy. Nor need we stress the dangers presented by these possibilities if they are acted upon by a totalitarian society. In this as in many other areas affecting our very identity as human beings, science and technology are relentlessly confronting us with decisions that will try all our resources of wisdom, restraint, flexibility, and courage.

Turning now to changes in the environment of intelligence that may influence its rate and range of development, we come closer to what common sense can conceive as feasible, although even here there are some radical possibilities opened up by advances in psychopharmacology. But the major environmental influences are obviously in the home, in the school, and in the communication process in society as a whole. We know from recent experimentation that language development can be greatly accelerated, and we may expect soon to have simple and economical mechanical devices for the acquisition of language and number skills at home and before formal schooling begins. The motivational variables are important here: even in culturally deprived segments of the population, individuals will soon have general access to the technical facilities that make for accelerated acquisition of skills and knowledge. The key to their use is the meaning they have to the persons concerned, to the value placed on the maximum development of intellectual capacities. It is probable that an increase of from 20 to 25 points in IQ between ages 4 and 7 can be produced by concentrated environmental enrichment in persons now among the culturally deprived. The crucial variables, apart from the essential motivational one, are such readily influenced factors as library facilities, books and periodicals in the home, availability of learning supplies (including autoinstructional devices), social support in providing learning outside the home as well as outside the school, opportunities for enlarging the vocabulary and for being in contact with persons who are models of good language usage (including popular heroes on TV), and a system of tangible rewards and recognition for achievement.

Among the ethnic groups whose members are prominently among the culturally deprived in the United States, the Negro presents a special problem. Social and historical conditions consequent upon slavery and a rather slow and still far from complete process of emancipation have resulted in a debasement of the potentiality of the Negro in America. There is no doubt that the opportunity exists here for some real experimentation in environmental modification and intervention. And we should build into every experimental program a method for appraising its effectiveness. We should certainly heed the call for action, but research geared both to short-term and long-term goals should be considered essential and given a high priority in the development of programs of social action. Galton's statement of the theoretical problem remains sound; what we need right now is thorough exploration of the effect of planned variations in environment, as well as of spontaneous changes in the naturally occurring environment, particularly in the area of *feelings*.

This latter aspect of "environment" needs especially to be stressed. The corrosive effect of racial hatred and rejection, especially of black by white and the more recently expressed reciprocal hatred of black for white, surely affects personal functioning in all areas of performance, including the use of intelligence to acquire the presented culture and to contribute to it. The very assumption that "intelligence" as defined by the ascendant group is a mark of intrinsic moral superiority is galling. It cannot be emphasized too much or said too often that intelligence as measured by intelligence tests is loaded with cultural value judgments, based primarily on the Judaic-Christian-European model of fit behavior. In brief, we must not forget the multifactorial nature of true intellect. Intelligence is *not* simply what our intelligence tests measure. Individuals who have suffered severe cultural deprivation are penalized relative to others by the limited nature of widely used measures; so too are the potentially creative. Persons with special sensibilities and talents that fit them for creative work in the arts, and to a lesser extent in science as well, are often underrated in terms of functional intelligence because of the personality and motivational factors associated with creativity, themselves part of the integral meaning of creative intellect.

Extensive developmental studies of the stability of creative thinking abilities, not only in the United States but in some half dozen other societies, have been carried out by Torrance (see Taylor, 1964). In these developmental studies, Torrance employed variants of the Guilford tests adapted for use with children ages 3 to 12. These included such verbal tests as Unusual Uses, Product Improvement, and the Ask-and-Guess Test, and three nonverbal tasks, Picture Completion, Incomplete Figures, and Circles. More than 6000 children were tested in various cultures (India, New Zealand, Australia, Germany, Norway, Western Samoa, and the United States) to obtain the developmental data. The sampling was made in kindergarten and from each grade level in grades one through six. Since the study was cross-sectional rather than longitudinal, stability of creativity in individual children cannot be estimated from the data. What is shown, however, is a steady rise of level of creative ability with age, though in some societies there were occasional puzzling reversals. In the United States, for example, at about age 9, near the end of the third grade or at the beginning of the fourth grade, there is a decrement instead of an increase. Torrance made a special study of classrooms in which the typical fourth-grade decline did *not* occur, and he found that in those cases the teacher had somehow eliminated this discontinuity by acting outside commonly accepted pedagogical procedures to stimulate the children's imaginations.

Despite the occasional reversal of growth noted in some schools, the conclusion seems warranted that creativity does increase with age much in the same way verbal intelligence does. The only fly in the ointment is the fact that the Torrance tests themselves show a small positive correlation with verbal intelligence, and it is possible that the verbal component alone is producing the increase of scores with age. In support of the Torrance conclusions, however, it might be noted that esthetic judgment, as Child (1967) has convincingly shown, also increases with age. The relationship of esthetic judgment to esthetic creativity is not definitely established, though our own findings with the Barron-Welsh Art Scale would support the view that more creative persons have better esthetic judgment. Certainly more developmental studies are needed, however.

The inheritance of esthetic judgment and of adaptive flexibility in the visual, figural sphere has recently been under study by the present writer through application of tests to an unselected sample of twins ages 16 to 18 in Italy. The study was carried out at the Institute for Medical Genetics in Florence and the Mendel Institute in Rome.[1]

In the twin method, evidence for the inheritance of a given characteristic is obtained by comparing the intraclass correlation in monozygotic (identical) twins with the correlation in dizygotic (fraternal) twins. In the present study, the subjects consisted of 59 pairs of like-sexed twins: 30 monozygotic pairs, 15 male and 15 female, and 29 dizygotic pairs, 14 male and 15 female. One of the DZ female pairs had to be excluded from the sample after testing because of incomplete data. The average age of the sample was 17; all were in secondary school at the time.

Zygosity diagnoses were arrived at from medical data, including blood tests, and one can assume they are highly accurate. All the twins had been studied since birth.

The tests selected for use were the Gottschaldt Figures Test, which in an earlier joint study by the present writer with Guilford and others was shown to have the highest loading of any test on the Adaptive Flexibility factor, and the Barron-Welsh Art Scale.

The results were as follows:

[1] Grateful acknowledgment is made to Drs. Luigi Gedda, Paolo Parisi, and H. Boutourline Young, without whose assistance the research could not have been accomplished. The study was supported financially by the Richardson Foundation.

1. Gottschaldt Figures (Adaptive Flexibility)

In this test, the task is to discover in a complex figure a simpler embedded one. Fifteen problems are presented. Scores ranged from 0 to 15, with a mean of 7.

The intraclass correlation in the monozygotic group is .86, in the dizygotic group, .35. Both correlations are significantly different from zero, and they are significantly different from one another as well (t of 4.79, p less than .01). A high degree of heritability for this factor is indicated; the Holzinger heritability coefficient is .78 (Holzinger, 1929).

2. Barron-Welsh Art Scale (Esthetic Judgment)

The correlation in the monozygotic group is .58; in the dizygotic group. .07. The MZ correlation is significantly different from zero, but the DZ is not; they are significantly different from one another (t of 3.05, p less than .01), and a high heritability component is indicated by the Holzinger heritability coefficient of .55. Whether what is inherited is a preference for complexity or a greater ability to discriminate in the esthetic realm is not altogether clear, however, as our earlier discussion of the Art Scale would imply.

For the entire sample of 118 subjects, the mean score on the Art Scale is 28, as compared with a mean of 14 for American high school groups, a highly significant difference. In view of the historical contribution of Italy to the arts, it seems possible that a higher than average level of esthetic discrimination may be carried in the Italian gene pool. Further studies to clarify these relationships are now in progress in a collaboration between the Institute of Personality Assessment and Research and the Harvard University Florence project, in which groups of Italian youth are being compared with the American-born offspring of Italian immigrants to the Boston area.

While these results are not unambiguous, especially in view of the uncertainties that attend twin studies in which environmental similarity is assumed, they do point to the likelihood at least that two factors important to creativity are inherited. This would support the recent research results from a study of twins in the National Merit Scholarship competition (Nichols, 1965). Nichols studied some 1500 pairs of twins who had taken the National Merit Scholarship Qualifying Test, which consists of five subtests: English Usage, Mathematics Usage, Social Studies Reading, Natural Science Reading, and Word Usage. Factor analysis showed that each subtest measures a general factor and also an ability specific to itself. A comparison of MZ and DZ twins revealed consistently higher intraclass correlations in the MZ group both for the general factor and specific subtest scores. Nichols concluded that heredity accounts for about 70 percent of the variance both in general ability and in the specific abilities measured by the test.

Thus, in a sense we are back where we started, before factor analysis began to challenge the assumption of unidimensionality of intelligence held by the early testmakers. Although intelligence is revealed to be factorially complex, some specific factors themselves, from the little evidence we have available to us thus far, appear quite possibly to be inherited. However, in a matter of such practical as well as theoretical importance, we need much more research evidence before coming to any conclusion.

Chapter Twelve

Nurturing and Encouraging Creativity

While in some respects creativity seems to be a hardy plant and even to flourish in the midst of hardship and privation, a developing body of testimony from educators and from psychologists in the school system suggests that much potential creativity is made to wither by an unfavorable climate both in the classroom and in society at large.

We have already had a look at some of the data of the Getzels-Jackson study, in which especially creative but relatively less intelligent, though still quite bright, pupils were less popular with teachers, and less in line with both teacher and peer value systems, than pupils whose IQs were relatively high as compared with their creativity. Although no evidence existed directly in the data, there was at least the implication that creativity was maintained at some cost to personal security, or that a special motive was required to sustain creativity in the face of its comparative devaluation by the immediately present representatives of society.

The Getzels-Jackson findings have been replicated in essential details by E. Paul Torrance and his associates at the University of Minnesota Bureau of Educational Research, in a series of studies at the University of Minnesota Laboratory Elementary School, a Minneapolis public high school, the University of Minnesota High School, and two graduate schools. They showed not only that creative thinking abilities contributed to academic achievement in a way that had not been properly appreciated, but that peer disapproval was just as potent a factor as teacher devaluation in driving divergent thinking underground.

It is interesting that the creative young women studied by Helson had themselves exhibited in childhood a tendency towards divergent thinking and a rejection of conventional feminine adjustment, although outright tomboyishness was only one of several possible creative patterns for them as girls (1967). On a Creative Activities Checklist, devised by Helson, the creative Mills College seniors, retrospecting on their childhood activities by way of the Helson 37-items list, differed significantly (at the .05 level or better) from the control group on the following listed activities: *writing poems and stories; painting, drawing, and working with clay; creating complex imaginary situations and acting in them;* and *reading.* They reported more frequently *putting on shows, hiking and exploring,* and *horseback riding,* although these differences did not quite reach significance. *Playing alone,* and *playing the piano or violin,* were included by Helson in addition to the first five items above in a "creative activities scale" which significantly differentiated the "creatives" from the control group and which also had significant correlations with the Independence of Judgment Scale, the CPI Originality Scale, and the Complexity Scale. Helson generalized the findings as showing "complex unstereotyped symbolic activity" as the characteristic difference between creative and uncreative girls; the latter more commonly preferred social play.

The relative lack of reward in the school system, as expressed in that most transferable of coinage, school grades, for creative intellectual ability was shown in another interesting study, this time of adolescents in a Michigan high school. Elizabeth Drews (1960) studied three groups who had been equated for intelligence: social leaders, studious achievers, and creative intellectuals, as revealed by interest and performance patterns in high school. The creative intellectuals received significantly lower teacher grades, and these were especially low in comparison with their actual scholastic achievement as evidenced in other accomplishments.

An impressive study in depth of the creative adolescent has been made by Emanuel Hammer, working with students of painting in the High School Scholarship Painting Workshop at New York University. The Workshop faculty, themselves painters of distinction, classified the students, 18 in all, into three categories: (1) merely facile and lacking in creativity and originality; (2) intermediate; and (3) truly creative, with a high degree of promise for serious painting. There were five students each in categories 1 and 3. While this is a very small number of cases, they were studied in such depth that the findings commend themselves to our attention as a serious preliminary exploration.

Hammer's findings, expressed in terms of the qualities of the genuinely creative young painters, are consistent at many points with the results both of the Institute's studies of creative adults and the studies of Torrance, Drews, and Getzels and Jackson with creative children and adolescents. The genuinely creative as opposed to merely facile young painters showed greater depth of feeling, stronger determination and ambition, independence, rebelliousness, tolerance of discomfort, greater need for self-expression as well as range of emotion, self-awareness, and an integration of feminine and masculine components in their natures.

Torrance's studies of developmental patterns throughout the elementary grades have made him especially alert to the damping effect of the school system upon creativity. Creative children in the first three grades, especially boys, often have a reputation among the other children for having "silly ideas," or "naughty ideas," or are thought of as "wild" by their teachers. By the end of the third grade they have usually learned to be evasive and to keep their thoughts to themselves, with a consequent loss of some of that precious spark of originality. The ninth and tenth years are a transitional period for most children, however—one of the several nodal points at which the child gets noticeably more "broken in" and learns to take the bit for society's sake, and hopefully for his own as well, of course. The dynamics of freedom and discipline, integration and diffusion, order and disorder, and expression and restraint become apposite to creativity most vividly at these crisis points in development.

Torrance has a number of recommendations for the school counselor in his dealing with creative children, which make sense for teachers and principals as well, and indeed can apply in a variety of situations in which a creative individual, child or adult, is experiencing difficulty. "Society is downright savage toward creative thinkers, especially when they are young," says Torrance, and recommends the following: (1) provide a refuge; (2) be a sponsor or patron if you possess power or prestige in the social subsystem that is exerting pressure; (3) help the creative individual *understand* his divergence and the good reason for it; (4) let him communicate his ideas by listening to him and helping him to get listened to by others; (5) make efforts to get his creative talent recognized and rewarded; and (6) help parents (superiors, the authorities, and so on) to understand him.

For the creative individual himself, Torrance also has some wise suggestions. The creative individual needs to recognize and esteem his own creativity; he needs to learn how to guard it from exploitation and abuse; he needs to know how to accept inevitable limitations in the environment while yet holding to his purposes and searching for opportunities for the expression of his talent. He also needs to learn how to cope with hardships and with failure, with anxieties and fears, and to avoid isolation and retreat; he perhaps needs to learn not to be more obnoxious than necessary. He must not in his own mind equate rebellion with delinquency, or be led from rebellion to senseless and categorical opposition to society; he must resist the idea that his divergence is a sign that he is mentally ill or a bad person; he must be able to integrate the masculine and the feminine in his nature and not sacrifice part of himself to the social stereotype of masculinity or femininity.

While this might seem a large order, it is clear from our own research findings that highly successful creative individuals have been able to do this, though mostly on their own. How many others of potential creativity have fallen by the wayside cannot be estimated as yet, but there seems little doubt that the loss is considerable. The remedy surely does not lie simply in school counseling, but in a change of spirit in the educational system and in society at large. As we shall see later, there are signs that change is in the offing.

One of the most important of the changes is occurring in the National Merit Scholarship Corporation, whose program of competitive scholarship awards has attracted much attention, quite out of proportion indeed to the amount of money involved in the 500 scholarships awarded each year. The establishment of a highly discriminating basis of selection has made the National Merit Scholarship a highly desirable one; it is a signal honor as well as a help to the struggling student. Recently, on the basis of research and recommendations by Holland and Kent (1960), the National Merit Scholarship administrators decided to make 25 scholarships each year available to candidates who could not qualify on high school grades or on standard scholastic aptitude tests but who had manifested a high level of creative ability in the sciences or the arts. Holland devised rating scales in which the following sorts of behaviors were recognized as having importance quite apart from grades or test-measured achievement:

Creative Science Scale

1. Presenting an original paper at a scientific meeting sponsored by a professional society

2. Winning a prize or award in a scientific talent search
3. Constructing scientific apparatus on own initiative
4. Inventing a patentable device
5. Having a scientific paper published in a science journal

Creative Arts Scale

1. Winning one or more speech contests
2. Having poems, stories, or articles published in a public newspaper or magazine or in a state or national high school anthology
3. Winning a prize or an award in an art competition (sculpture, ceramics, painting, and so forth)
4. Receiving the highest rating in a state music contest
5. Receiving one of the highest ratings in a national music contest
6. Composing music that is performed at least once in public
7. Arranging music for a public performance
8. Having at least a minor role in plays (not high-school or church-sponsored)
9. Having leads in high-school or church-sponsored plays
10. Winning a literary award or prize for creative writing
11. Having a cartoon published in a public newspaper or magazine

Certainly the provision of social recognition and reward for creative endeavor is one effective way of endorsing it and increasing the valuation placed upon it by society. The late President Kennedy lent the prestige of his high office to this sort of social endorsement of creativeness, not only through hospitality extended at the White House to great creators in the arts and sciences, but also through the emphasis he gave to the selection of recipients for the Medal of Freedom and, in innumerable less public acts, to the encouragement of flexible and original thinking in all kinds of projects touching upon our national life.

Chapter Thirteen

Increasing Individual Creativity through Special Educational Experiences

But quite apart from nurturing and rewarding the creativity that has sprung up more or less on its own, can we do anything to increase it in ourselves and others by education, training, or selected unusual experience? Since we are getting more and more information about the factors involved, can we begin to devise programs that will strengthen creative thinking abilities and reduce the effect of inhibiting circumstances? Is our knowledge useful knowledge, in the sense that it leads to prediction and control?

Two of the earliest efforts at application were brainstorming and synectics, the former the idea of Alex Osborn, the latter a system of training devised by William J. J. Gordon for industrial inventors. Both have a slightly artificial flavor to them, although this first impression disappears when one examines them closely. The interpretation of them as gimmicks probably comes from the fact that they were packaged to sell to industry and sometimes were made to sound like a new mechanical device to step up the output from tired Research and Development brains. We choose them for discussion here simply as representatives of programs of training; throughout the country there are a number of programs with similar emphases.

Brainstorming in all seriousness has been taught in recent years most notably by Sidney J. Parnes, whose article "Do You Really Understand Brainstorming?" (1962) is refreshing and clarifying. He points out that brainstorming is essentially part of a total process; creative problem solving is the whole, brainstorming is an element that is usually present whether one sets it up deliberately or not. The basic property of the brainstorm is the outpouring of ideas *without evaluation while the storm is on.* The critical faculty tends to slow down the rate of production of ideas and to reduce them in quantity in a given space of time. It might be clearer, Parnes suggests, if one spoke simply of a *principle of deferred judgment* while ideas were allowed to spring freely to mind and combinatorial play was encouraged in order to increase quantity.

Thus understood, brainstorming is equally applicable to individual thinking as to the group technique that made the term and the method popular. The four rules of brainstorming in a group are: (1) adverse criticism is taboo; (2) freewheeling is welcomed; (3) quantity is wanted; and (4) combination and improvement are sought. Although there have been some studies (for example, Taylor, Berry, and Block, 1957) which call into question the claim that group brainstorming results in the production of more ideas per unit time than individual conventional problem-solving techniques, the majority of controlled investigations do show an increase in both quantity and quality. It must be remembered, however, that only certain kinds of problems can be approached through such a method, and that when the problem itself requires a high level of integral intellect applied to a vast range of details in a search for a resolving explanation, the *whole* process of creative problem solving is called into play.

A recognition of this integrating quality in the creative act gives to "synectics" some depth as a method. The word means "the joining together of different and apparently irrelevant elements."

It too began as a group method, its intention being to integrate diverse individuals into a problem-stating and problem-solving group; like brainstorming, however, its fundamental rules or principles of operation are equally applicable to problem solving by an individual. Its aim is to increase awareness of the mechanisms through which one arrives at novel solutions; one goal, therefore, is to gain insight into the underlying process itself as it occurs, either in the group or the individual, and then to arrange the most suitable circumstances for the emergence of novelty.

Synectics in operation depends heavily on two mechanisms: making the strange familiar, and making the familiar strange. The first of these is the search for similarity; confronted with a new problem, we ask ourselves whether it is not an old problem, had we but the wit to see it. Seeing even partial resemblances may lead to the application of familiar methods in solving the new problem.

Making the familiar strange is a way of shedding preconceptions and perceptual habits. Innocence of vision, a certain naïveté, and ingenuousness, characterize the creative individual; if these qualities can be cultivated, the novelty of invention and problem solution should be increased. Problem stating especially is dependent on this sort of naïveté; one of the worst effects of habit is to blind us even to the fact that a problem exists. (We are so habituated to the idea of death, for instance, that medicine hardly asks the question, Can death be prevented?, but asks only, How can life be prolonged? One might reasonably expect such a problem to be insoluble even if stated, but a priori improbability of solution may not be the reason for its not being stated.)

To attain these goals of making the familiar strange and the strange familiar, synectics employs four main methods: personal analogy, direct analogy, symbolic analogy, and fantasy. Examples of personal analogy given by Gordon (1961) are: Faraday "looked into the very heart of the electrolyte endeavoring to render the play of its atom visible to his mental eyes"; Kekule identified himself with a snake swallowing its tail, and saw thereby an analogy to the benzene molecule as possibly a ring rather than a chain of carbon atoms. Personal analogy there merges into direct analogy. As an example of direct analogy: Alexander Graham Bell writes of his invention of the telephone,

> It struck me that the bones of the human ear were very massive, indeed, as compared with the delicate thin membranes that operated them, and the thought occurred that if a membrane so delicate could move bones relatively so massive, why should not a thicker and stouter piece of membrane move my piece of steel . . . and the telephone was conceived.

Symbolic analogy, as Gordon describes it, is usually a visual image, disembarrassed of words yet immediate and poetic. It is especially valuable to the inventor because a complex visual resolution fitting a number of requirements is the inventor's product. An example from Gordon is: "How to invent a jacking mechanism to fit a box not bigger than four by four inches yet extend out and up three feet and support four tons?" The solution began to develop when a group member suggested the Indian rope trick as a symbolic analogy "The rope is soft when the guy starts with it . . . the magic is how he makes it hard so he can climb up on it . . ." A few intermediate symbolic analogies led onward to the solution: the hydraulic principle of erection of the penis, and analogy then to a steel tape measure, then to a bicycle chain with flexible links that stiffened as they were driven out of the jacking mechanism.

Biological analogies, frequently including the sexual, were found most useful by the synectics group in the development of new products. Many mechanical devices are direct analogies to the form and function of the human body; the machine is an extension of human might built on the human model.

Fantasy is used in synectics as a way of freeing the imagination from the bounds of the given world. Specific physical laws are imagined not to hold—what would be the consequences? The procedure is very much like the Guilford Consequences test itself, which in turn was based upon Bennett's Productive Thinking Test. The latter was used at the Institute of Personality Assessment and Research in 1950 in our first study of originality in graduate students, and when scored for "cosmicality" and "originality" it proved to be an excellent predictor of faculty ratings of Originality. The reader is referred again to "An Odd Fellow" for some examples of original and more or less cosmic responses in that type of test situation.

We ourselves found Gordon's techniques quite useful in a training and research program with teachers and principals in the Goleta, California, public schools. The immediate goal of the program was to increase creative thinking in the teachers and principals themselves; the long-term goal was to enhance creative thinking in the students by changing the entire school climate through changes in the teachers and the administration.

This holistic strategy, with its emphasis on starting the process of change in the school system by getting teachers and administrators *to change themselves*, is critically important. The educational establishment as a whole, like many social institutions, tends to develop into a closed system, to stick with established methods, to play it safe even in the face of evidence that new needs are coming into being and that old methods fail to meet these needs. Unfortunately, the closed institutional system tends to make the people within it into its own image, so that they too become "closed people." To stimulate creative change, we must begin with *the psychodynamics of the individual*.

I might add that this approach to the teacher *as a person* has the advantage of engaging attention, interest, and commitment from the teacher. The teachers we worked with, almost without exception, became intensely involved in the process. This is very important, for the failure of many innovations in curriculum can be traced to the neglect of a strategy for introducing teachers to the innovation and keeping them committed to it, both intellectually and emotionally.

The director of the Goleta program was George I. Brown, a professor of education at the University of California at Santa Barbara; I was called in as a planning consultant. Brown and I decided on a method of approach that would combine living-in assessment with a sort of semitherapeutic personal relationship with the teachers. The living-in assessment was defined not as "assessment" but as "a retreat."

This first "retreat" was held in a secluded spot in the hills east of Santa Barbara, in an old country inn. A group of speakers representing rather diverse interests and professions was assembled for this weekend meeting with the teachers and principals. Each was asked to speak to the question of the importance of imagination and creativity in human affairs. One was a prominent California jurist, who startled the audience by proposing new and imaginative approaches to the problems of marijuana use, prostitution, and usury; in effect, he proposed making all three legal, though with various social controls. Another speaker, Dr. James T. Lester, Jr., was a member of the American expedition that had recently completed an ascent of Mount Everest. He showed photographs of the climb and developed the thesis that the resources of imagination had been as important as courage and mountaineering skills in making the expedition a success. He concluded by showing photographs of the Sherpa guides in a journey by automobile across the United States (with him as chauffeur), using their delighted reactions to new experiences as an example of the joyousness of discovery and exploration.

These and other speakers were deliberately chosen to help set a tone of unconventionality, freedom from routine, and a certain amount of positive-toned daring as important to real efforts at change.

This first retreat was attended by teachers, principals, superintendents, and members of interested departments on the University of California campus. It was thought of as "the kick-off," to get the game started and to let people get acquainted with one another. Three smaller weekend meetings were then scheduled, one for each school. An important feature of these meetings was the participation of the principal, who took part in the "assessments" on an equal basis with the teachers. A battery of personality tests was administered, including the Minnesota Multiphasic and the California Psychological Inventory. Each participant was interviewed twice, once concerning his personal life history, and once on his experiences in his teaching career. Particular attention in the latter interview was given to the teacher's philosophy of teaching and to experiences that had been particularly rewarding or particularly distressing. Each was especially questioned about what kinds of students he liked or disliked, and he was asked to describe real students and to give concrete examples of behavior.

Five tests were selected for use in appraising the effectiveness of the year's program: the Barron-Welsh Art Scale, the Barron Complexity of Outlook Scale, and three tests from the Guilford battery: Alternate Uses, Consequences, and Plot Titles, scored for high quality responses. These were given at the first assessments in October and the last in June. Scores on these tests were not revealed to the participants until the year's work was completed.

As part of the strategy of engaging the personal interest of the participants, we decided to feed back the results of the personality tests at Retreat No. 3, held about one month after Retreat No. 2 for each school. This was done with each teacher or principal individually, and with proper assurances that the transaction would be confidential. The participants were given the actual scores on the personality tests, in the form of test profiles, and the metric and rationale of the tests were explained. Then their own scores were discussed with them at length, without, however, any implication that the tests were "the truth" about them as persons. They were encouraged, in fact, to disagree wth the test results if they felt they were invalid.

A total of 29 teachers and administrators took part in this aspect of the research. Significant gains were registered on all the measures of performance hypothesized to be related to creativity. For the Barron-Welsh Art Scale, pre- and post-program test scores analyzed by the Wilcoxon matched-pairs signed-ranks test showed a T score of 65.5, significant beyond the .005 level. A similar level of significance was demonstrated for differences in scores on the Complexity of Outlook Scale. The Guilford tests were analyzed for differences in mean scores before and after the program, and on both Alternate Uses and Consequences, scored both for low quality (Ideational Fluency) and high quality (Originality), statistically significant differences were found. (It should be added, however, that the average increment was relatively slight, ranging from 10 to 15 percent. In retrospect we felt that tests such as these, with their characteristic emphasis on very close timing and rather brief work intervals for each problem, were not the instruments of choice, for the range of possible change for subjects who have been highly motivated to perform at first testing is rather limited.)

It is of some interest to look at the personality patterns associated with favorable or unfavorable response to this sort of program. I shall therefore present the personality test reports of the two teachers who showed the least change in terms of the measures of creativity we used as criteria, and then the test reports of the two who made the most conspicuous gains. These reports were written immediately after the initial testing and are "blind" interpretations of the test profiles, given without any other information about the person except age, sex, and occupation. The MMPI and the CPI were considered together in formulating a psychodynamic diagnosis.

"No Change" Case No. 1

MMPI–CPI. This 44-year-old woman is not without her problems. She appears quite constricted and somewhat compulsive, and in mood is probably chronically depressed. The depression could get out of hand, and there is the possibility of a serious involutional state in the next few years. With good environmental support, however, she probably will go along much as she is now, somewhat down at the mouth and somewhat unsociable and retiring, but meeting her responsibilities well in a highly conforming yet not seriously rigid manner. She has a certain amount of flexibility and insight, as well as a reasonable amount of tolerance. She probably is plagued by a host of minor physical ailments and may feel tired a great deal of the time. In her quiet way she is feminine and probably rather nurturant in her relationship with the children in school.

"No Change" Case No. 2

MMPI–CPI. This 45-year-old man is a highly responsible, stable, conventional, slightly rigid individual, perhaps a bit too "good" for his own good, yet withal an effective model of probity for the young. He appears to be somewhat passive, and he could conceivably have a problem in sexual identity (with fantasies and near-action impulses coming into the picture occasionally). He is so conscientious, however, and also so suppressed, that one would not expect any overt pathology. He is likely to be nurturant, perhaps even motherly, in his attitude towards the boys he teaches. The psychic cost to him of the defenses he must maintain is fairly heavy. A chronic mild depression is likely. He can also swing towards paranoia easily, although his expression of it would be muted. He is quite self-critical. In general, he can be described as a deferent, self-abasing, fearful individual, lacking in assertiveness, who gets along by being orderly, obedient, cautious, openly dependent on others, supportive of the status quo, and the enemy of no one.

"Conspicuous Change" Case No. 1

MMPI–CPI. This energetic, active, rather self-possessed 25-year-old woman is highly participative socially in a gay and sometimes superficial and frivolous manner. She is sensitive and insightful, able and indeed willing to think easily in terms of psychological motivation. She herself is psychodynamically complex, with much going on beneath a facade of carefree, almost irresponsible sociability. Insofar as there is a problem which might be manifested as a clinical symptom, it would center upon sexual identity; she is somewhat masculine in interest pattern, markedly so for this group of women, yet she is not a dominant or masterful person. She might manifest occasional social delinquency, although not of a harmful sort; she is somewhat impulsive, but not mean, and in fact is quite accepting of others and very tolerant in her attitudes. Her ego strength is excellent, and she appears to be basically well adjusted.

"Conspicuous Change" Case No. 2

MMPI–CPI.   This 47-year-old man is a notably stable and effective individual, yet he is markedly lacking in self-esteem. He is temperate and deliberate in manner, does not like to push himself, and would easily be underrated at first meeting. He is quite astute in his psychological evaluations of others, notably flexible and independent, and unobtrusively efficient. His responsibility and self-control make him someone to rely on over the long haul. He conforms easily, but he clearly values independence and a certain amount of criticism of social norms, and he himself is basically an independent thinker in spite of his manner and general style of representing himself. He has more sympathy for social deviance than one might expect. Why his self-esteem is low is the most important question one can ask about him. This is holding him back. He needs assurance, but exactly what would be reassuring is not clear. He probably knows consciously that he's quite capable. The matter would probably be worth his exploring in depth.

Professor Brown is continuing to work along these same lines, although with even more emphasis on "depth" techniques, including dream analysis by the Gestalt therapy method of Fritz Perls and sensory awareness and encounter group training. This latter work is being carried on in collaboration with the Esalen Institute, which now provides the "away from home" setting for the weekend retreats. My own work with the Santa Barbara

Project ended after one year as I left that summer for the first step in the research in Ireland described earlier.

The success of the senior teachers' program was demonstrated not only by significant gains in test performance but also by the behavior and feelings of the teachers. While no systematic attempt was made to observe classroom behavior, both teachers and principals gave convincing anecdotal accounts of changes in the teacher-student relationship. The teachers were interviewed not only at the end of the school year, but also at the beginning of the succeeding year, after a summer in which many of them participated in the Head Start program. The present writer conducted both the assessment interviews and the later interviews. A repeated theme in the end-of-summer interviews was that the teachers found themselves better able to relate empathically with the culturally deprived children, most of whom were from Mexican-American families in which English was not commonly used at home. The creativity training program had stressed empathy both with other people and with nonhuman parts of the environment. (One of the techniques that the children especially liked was an exercise in which they were to imagine what it felt like to be a misspelled word.)

It was encouraging to see that the program could produce change in teachers and principals already part of the school system. The teachers who responded well to the program were those who were more "open" to begin with; as with formal psychotherapy, those who are better off at the start are better able to use the process to effect desired changes.

In the weekly sessions with senior teachers, Brown employed a theoretical approach he had earlier used successfully in teacher training at the undergraduate level, involving identification of a "sub-self" with a fictionalized symbol of creativity. An especially effective children's story book used in this project is *Some Very Nice Things* by J. Merrill and R. Solbert. It tells the story of William Elephant and Old Owl, who find "some very nice things" washed up on a desert island they are inhabiting; the very nice things are a shirt, pants, gloves, and a hat. William Elephant proceeds to put the things to unusual uses, making a trunk-warmer out of one of the gloves, for example, and a sail for a home-made boat out of the shirt. Elephant's ideas are scorned by Old Owl, who acts for all the world like the peer groups in Torrance's studies who discourage creativity. Children, and teachers as well for that matter, can be taught to adopt Elephant's frame of mind and reject Owl's, with a consequent increase in originality. In fact, in two studies with teacher candidates, Brown (1965a; 1965b) found significant increases in both the Barron-Welsh Art Scale and the Complexity Scale when Ss were asked to take the tests as though they were William Elephant.

Covington and Crutchfield (1965) have attacked the problem of training by constructing a special curriculum in creative problem solving, using an autoinstructional program. To assess it they gave tests of creativity to an experimental group (98 fifth- and sixth-grade pupils who experienced the special training) and a matched control group of 97 elementary school students who experienced simply the standard curriculum. They found that the special training did in fact result in an impressive increase in creativity. Three kinds of criterion measures were employed by Crutchfield and Covington, all tests being administered before the training period began and again at its conclusion. The criterion measures were as follows:

1. Complex problem-solving tasks without a time limit (the respondent is asked to think of ways in which a man could get himself out of a deep pit without using any tools; or, he is asked to solve the mysterious disappearance of a jewel from a darkened room; or, he is asked to explain what might have brought to an end the life of a city buried in the sand thousands of years ago; and so on).

2. The "divergent thinking" tests devised by Torrance (1962) for use with children (think of ways to make a toy truck "more fun to play with" e.g.).

3. Attitude tests (valuation of creative thinking and problem solving, self-confidence in own creative abilities, and so on).

The autoinstructional program itself consisted of a series of simplified detective and mystery stories. Each lesson presented a mystery and then gave a succession of clues and relevant information, each step in disclosure being preceded by a requirement that the child restate the problem in his own words and offer ideas to solve the mystery. Feedback to the child's responses was given on following pages of the autoinstructional booklet in the form of examples of ideas or questions he might have thought of.

An important feature of this procedure was the fact that the autoinstructional booklet was in the form of a cartoon or comic strip that seems to be telling of the adventures of a boy and girl, Jim and Lila, just the right ages to be in fifth or sixth grade, who are learning to be detectives by taking lessons from their uncle. Jim and Lila gradually come up with more and more unusual ideas, and they learn to evaluate them. The child reading the cartoon booklet is thus led to identify with children who think creatively and have a lot of fun doing so. (Who would not like to be a child detective?)

The impressive early findings in the Crutchfield and Covington research were corroborated on first cross-validation in the same school system, but an interesting decline in effectiveness of the training program occurred when the booklets were made available to a distant school system where they were simply handed out for use without any special effort to motivate the teachers and students (personal communication, Richard S. Crutchfield). Even though teaching devices are autoinstructional, it remains true that the learner may vary in motivation to use them. (After all, a book is about as good an autoinstructional device as has ever been invented, but it is of no use if nobody wants to read it.) A special virtue of the Crutchfield and Covington demonstration is that it was made within the school system itself and resulted in the development of techniques that can be incorporated into existing curricula.

In view of what has been said about the integral quality of creative intellect, one may wonder whether such experiments and such training programs with teachers and students produce lasting change. In Brown's experiments as well as in those of Covington and Crutchfield, only a short time has elapsed between the training program and the appraisal of changes.

It would be easy enough, therefore, to dismiss such results as superficial changes, but there may be more to the matter than that. The year-long program with adult teachers and principals was considered by all concerned to have resulted in important changes not only in the classroom but also, in many cases, in the daily living of the teachers themselves. A deep-seated personal process had occurred—or so it seemed to the clinical interviewer.

This question of depth or superficiality is a question that runs through all efforts to appraise behavior change, whether or not the theory itself claims depth of understanding, as psychoanalysis does, as well as depth of intervention. Synectics is explicit in aiming at the preconscious in an effort to stimulate the rate and complexity of combinations there through the use of metaphor, symbol, and fantasy. Psychoanalysis in a sense also seeks to broaden the sphere of influence of the preconscious, specifically, through intervention in the unconscious, by freeing energy that is being used uneconomically in the neurosis to keep ideational representations of tabooed and repressed drives "bound" in the unconscious. Kubie (1958) has argued that the creative process is interfered with, and distorted by, neurotic complexes and conflicts, and according to the psychoanalytic understanding of the unconscious, he is right.

But when artists speak of the unconscious as the source or wellspring of creativity, as many have convincingly done, they mean by unconscious a potentiality that is hardly personal at all, and certainly is not the "personal repressed." D. H. Lawrence, in his short monograph *Psychoanalysis and the Unconscious* (1961), puts the matter as clearly as it has been put analytically; Maritain says much the same thing as Lawrence, though more poetically as well as analytically, in *Creative Intuition in Art and Poetry*:

Reason does not only consist of its conscious logical tools and manifestations, nor does the will consist only of its deliberate conscious determinations. Far beneath the sunlit surface thronged with explicit concepts and judgments, words and expressed resolutions or movements of the will, are the sources of knowledge and creativity, of love and suprasensuous desires, hidden in the primordial translucid night of the intimate vitality of the soul. Thus it is that we must recognize the existence of an unconscious or preconscious which pertains to the spiritual powers of the human soul and to the inner abyss of personal freedom, and of the personal thirst and striving for knowing and seeing, grasping and expressing: a spiritual or musical unconscious which is specifically different from the automatic or deaf unconscious.

When man seeking for his own inner universe takes the wrong road, he enters the internal world of the deaf unconscious, while believing he enters the internal world of the spirit, and he thus finds himself wandering in a false kind of self-interiority, where wildness and automatism mimic freedom.

Maritain also says:

My contention, then, is that everything depends, in the issue we are discussing, on the recognition of the existence of a spiritual unconscious, or rather, preconscious, of which Plato and the ancient wise men were well aware, and the disregard of which in favor of the Freudian unconscious alone is a sign of the dullness of our times. There are two kinds of unconscious, two great domains of psychological activity screened from the grasp of consciousness: the preconscious of the spirit in its living springs, and the unconscious of blood and flesh, instincts, tendencies, complexes, repressed images and desires, traumatic memories, as constituting a closed or automatic dynamic whole. I would like to designate the first kind of unconscious by the name of *spiritual* or, for the sake of Plato, *musical unconscious* or preconscious; and the second by the name of automatic unconscious or *deaf unconscious*—deaf to the intellect, and structured into a world of its own apart from the intellect; we might also say, in quite a general sense, leaving aside any particular theory, *Freudian unconscious*.

These two kinds of unconscious life are at work at the same time; in concrete existence their respective impacts on conscious activity ordinarily interfere or intermingle in a greater or less degree; and, I think, never—except in some rare instance of supreme spiritual purification—does the spiritual unconscious operate without the other being involved, be it to a very small extent. But they are essentially distinct and thoroughly different in nature.

This idea of a *musical unconscious* squares well with accounts both of creative transport and of mystical experience, although, as Maritain notes, only rarely, if ever, is any human experience utterly free of influences from the personal-historical or Freudian unconscious. Perhaps this may explain some of the puzzlement we are left with when we try to understand either creative genius or rare religious experience. Freud tackled Dostoevski with the tools of psychoanalysis (*Dostoevski and Parricide,* 1952), and indeed made some progress in relating the themes of crime and punishment, or imagined parricide and self-sought expiation of guilt, in Dostoevski's personal life as well as in his greatest novels; yet Freud confessed when he offered us the results of his speculation that "before the problem of the creative artist analysis must, alas, lay down its arms." The more credit to Freud for doing so, however, and, if we do adopt the designation "Freudian unconscious" for the sphere of mental influence that he investigated so brilliantly, we should do so as one names a new land in honor of its discoverer and explorer, or perhaps as one names a disease in honor of the physician who described its workings and helped conquer it.

Berdyaev has taken quite a different approach to Dostoevski, one that pays heed precisely to the musical unconscious before which Freud lay down his arms. To read the two works together is to see immediately, in the light of three geniuses, these two very different sorts of unconscious mental life. And for some further light reading, nothing could be better than two of Balzac's last works, *Louis Lambert* and *Seraphita* (1907), the first of which shows us Balzac's own tortured inquiry into the two sorts of unconscious as they bear upon the renunciation of sexuality, and the second of which tells of the final embodiment, in both male and female form, of a spirit on the very edge of "supreme purification." Balzac gives us for good measure in the latter story an interior essay on Emanuel Swedenborg, himself one of the great psychological puzzles in whom the Freudian unconscious and the musical or spiritual unconscious are almost inextricably mixed.

In the following chapter we shall consider some of the more profound, and potentially dangerous or upsetting, methods for studying the creative unconscious and for arousing it to participation in the more common round of everyday life and thought.

Chapter Fourteen

Creativity
and Altered States
of Consciousness

There are various methods of inducing an altered state of consciousness in which aspects of reality to which one usually does not have access suddenly become prominent because of changes in the very mode of experiencing. The methods themselves, or prototypes of them, are described concisely in two books by Aldous Huxley (1964), *The Doors of Perception* and *Heaven and Hell* (the latter an allusion, perhaps, to Swedenborg's monumental work, in reply to which William Blake had written "The Marriage of Heaven and Hell" [1926], one of the germinal contributions to a theory of the creative process). The main methods, some of which may sound modern but all of which in basic idea are ancient, are these: (1) breathing of carbon dioxide in a specially prepared mixture consisting of seven parts of oxygen to three parts of carbon dioxide; (2) exposure with eyes open to the rhythmic flashing of a stroboscopic lamp; (3) fasting (either general fasting or abstention from specific foods); (4) bodily mortification, such as self-flagellation; (5) ingestion of naturally occurring substances whose active chemical ingredients produce changes in consciousness, such as the peyote cactus.

The ancients, without scientific knowledge of physiological causation, used practices equivalent to some of these, such as Yogic breathing exercises which by way of prolonged suspension of breathing produce high carbon dioxide concentrations in the blood. Hypoxia will produce the same effects, and perhaps some of the mystical qualities attributed to an ascent to mountain heights for meditation are due actually to a decreased proportion of oxygen in the air and hence via decreased oxygen intake to an increase in carbon dioxide concentration. Prolonged rhythmic shouting, singing, and dancing may also produce this effect, and perhaps these have something in common as well with the methods that depend on rhythmic alternations in neural stimulation. Fasting may produce vitamin deficiencies, such disorders as scurvy and pellagra have long been known to generate negative affects of a quasi-mystical sort. Adrenalin metabolism and low blood sugar have also been implicated in accounts of unusual psychic states. And the peyote cactus, of course, is the source of mescaline, one of the more potent hallucinogenic drugs along with psilocybin and LSD-25.

The mediating mechanism in purely psychological terms may be simply a common mode of action physiologically, producing as the most noticeable effect an alteration of perceptual constancies. These are manifestations at the perceptual level of the principle of homeostasis. The central nervous system acts in an adaptive fashion not only by the production of relevant behaviors which help maintain the organism's integrity against environmental dangers, but also in an eliminative fashion by restricting the possible input to consciousness from the great variety of stimuli which are either irrelevant to our efficient functioning or potentially harmful to it.

Both the human organism's capacity to integrate stimuli, and the individual human being's personal history of "learning to see," are involved in the eliminative or selective function in the service of homeostasis. Seeing in the adult is largely a process of recognizing those signs in the environment which have been proved by his individual experience to be important for maintaining his biological and psychological being in integral form. In brief, we learn to identify, in the very process of receiving stimulation, those aspects of the sensory process that correspond to important aspects of our inner and outer environments. When our "education" is more or less complete, we bring to the act of seeing a large assortment of selective perceptual schemata, most of proven adaptive value. The hallucinogenic drugs in particular appear to act centrally upon the faculty of conscious attention in such fashion as to render these perceptual schemata, or constancies—in sum, the normalizing and adaptive apparatus of the ego—temporarily inoperative or at least substantially abrogated.

The hallucinogenic drugs exercised an initial appeal for these purposes because they were quite powerful and, during the first half of this century, easy to obtain legally if one knew of them at all. The early literature stressed the mystical experience produced by substances such as peyote. As LSD became more popularly known during the 1950's and the early 1960's it quite drove out of the market the older nondrug methods that take a lot of time and require suffering and spiritual discipline as a prelude to "the supreme purification." It is easy to be skeptical of them for this reason and to make fun of them, as the "instant Zen" tag does in appreciation of their meeting the typically American demand for quick results. But if the cortex is the repository of potentialities which we as individuals have had little or nothing to do with, why should we need to suffer individually to gain access to a potential nature that is our evolutionary legacy and for which we ourselves as individuals provide a vehicle for man's journey into the future? Further, who is to measure suffering in terms of time, and how do we know that the drugs are a shortcut? Perhaps one can gain from them only what one can suffer in the brief span of their action . . . perhaps they enable us to suffer more . . . to "die unto ourself" . . . so might the reply run.

That they can also lead into a wild ride in the deaf unconscious (J. Maritain's phrase), an automatic jig of horrors that may simulate freedom but is actually automatism, is incontrovertible. Unmistakably psychotic states have occurred as a result of ingestion of the hallucinogenic drugs, and in some cases these psychoses have proved long-lasting and resistant to treatment. The hallucinogens are unquestionably dangerous, as almost anything so powerful can be. In a certain percentage of cases, perhaps 1 in 100, given unfavorable predisposing circumstances in the individual or in the surrounding circumstances at the time the drug is taken, the hallucinogenic drugs may lead to unconstructive mental imbalance and actual breakdown of ego functions rather than temporary abrogation of them. Control based on understanding is the key to their constructive use, as it is to the use of other energy sources, such as fire or nuclear energy or the rush and pressure of water. (See Barron, Jarvik, and Bunnell, 1964.)

When the hallucinogens *are* used carefully and with understanding, what are the effects that have led some investigators to think they may be useful in increasing creativity? The following list of reported effects is drawn from numerous subjective reports in writing by individuals who have taken mescaline, LSD-25, or psilocybin. The whole range of effects does not occur on every occasion, but those given here are reported repeatedly and even though not invariant may be considered typical.

1. INTENSIFICATION OF ESTHETIC SENSIBILITY. Colors become more vivid and glowing; the play of light on objects is enchanting; surface details become sharply defined; sensual harmonies, of sound, light, color become marked. There are beautiful synesthesias, in which patterns of association usually confined to a single sense modality may cross over to others: music is "heard" as colored light, for example.

In some cases, ugliness will become intensified. A garish light may seem horrible, an unmusical sound unbearable; a false tone in a human voice may seem like a shriek; a false expression on a face may make it into a grotesque mask.

Both beauty and ugliness in objects thus are more than usually important and the esthetic qualities of the perceived world take on much greater value.

2. UNUSUAL ASSOCIATIONAL PATTERNS ARE MUCH MORE FRE-
QUENT. Much as in the synectics technique when it works, the
familiar can become quite strange. One may look at a familiar
object as though seeing it for the first time. Perceptual habits drop
away; hidden essences seem to reveal themselves. Analogical and
symbolic properties of persons, events, and objects come into the
foreground and combine to produce meaning and pattern where
none was seen before.

3. INTUITION IN RELATION TO OTHER PEOPLE IS INCREASED.
Other people, whether they themselves are under the influence of
the drug or not, are "seen through," though not ncessarily in a
negative sense. One subject wrote: "The faces of other people became clear and beautiful and open. . . . I could look at them without fear or shyness. . . . People looked naked, shed of a fog of
dissimulations, anxieties, hypocrisies. Everyone was true to his
own self and no one was ashamed."

Again, however, there can be a negative aspect to this.
Intuition is a risky way of understanding others; it can result in
brilliant successes or in almost incredible misapprehensions. It
proceeds by seizing upon striking details at the expense of other
details and making a sort of theory on very limited evidence on
the basis simply of "fit." Fictional amateur detectives in the
Sherlock Holmes tradition made intuition their stock in trade, and
of course they were always right. But when the intuitive approach
fails, it can be spectacularly wrong.[1] So far as the hallucinogenic

---

[1] In an anonymous novel, *The Smiling Corpse,* a master of detective fiction
turned the tables on such colleagues as G. K. Chesterton, Sax Rohmer,
Dashiell Hammett, and S. S. Van Dyne by imagining them at a literary tea
during the course of which the host is found murdered. The authors proceed
in the fashion of their fictional detective heroes to solve the murder, each
quite ingeniously by mutually contradictory theories, all of which of course
are wrong. Sax Rohmer, for instance, knowing that there is an Ancient
Order of the Purple Toes in Japan, and finding (by ingenious means) that
the Japanese houseboy's toes are painted purple, proceeds to accumulate
much circumstantial evidence that implicates the houseboy, who proves em-
barrassingly enough to have athlete's foot which he is treating with potassium permangamate. And so on . . .

drugs are concerned, we can say with assurance that they increase
the use of intuition and so increase one factor in creativity; but
sober judgment is the final arbiter of the validity of the intuitive
leap.

4. HIGHER PURPOSES AND THE MOTIVATION TO MAKE ONE'S LIFE
PHILOSOPHICALLY MEANINGFUL BECOME VERY IMPORTANT. Tri-
vial motives, pretenses, social "games" are seen as distractions
from the true business of life. One's own life and meaning may be
meditated upon, and a new appraisal *sub specie aeternitatis* may
be made. Thus, profound motivational change in the direction of
dedicating one's life to a higher purpose may come about. The
ordinary round of life will no longer do.

This too may have troublesome consequences, it need hardly
be added. For one thing, it upsets other people, who can no
longer count upon one's more mundane motives. Changes of this
sort in motivational structure may result in ruptures in personal
relations, work relations, financial arrangements, as well as general social behavior. If in this new cosmic scale of things one's life
seems intolerably empty and too far gone to change, there may be
impulses toward self-destruction or cessation of the known self.
(For a profound discussion of the desire for cessation, see Edwin
Shneidman's essay [1963] in *The Study of Lives.*)

5. A MYSTICAL EXPERIENCE OF ABSOLUTE FREEDOM MAY OC-
CUR. This is perhaps not so frequent a phenomenon as to deserve
to be called typical, but it occurs often enough in persons under
the influence of hallucinogenic drugs to warrant remark; and as a
source of motivational change it is by all odds the most powerful
of all. In it, the personal ego seems utterly dissolved, and the
individual has his existence in the grounds of being itself. The
experience is of "the void"; that is, the "abyss" of which philosophers have spoken. Without entering into the metaphysics of the
matter, we can say as psychologists that the individual who has
had this experience emerges from it with a sense of inner freedom

and power, although as usual there may be a negative as well as a positive aspect to this. In the negative case, the freedom seems based on a sense of nonbeing, on identification with a final nothingness. Heidigger (1929) has expressed this interpretation of freedom as having its ground in nonbeing most vividly, perhaps, in his *Beyond Metaphysics*; and it may be no accident that he was a supporter of Nazism. The writings of Jakob Boehme offer a more inclusive formulation in which both the positive and the negative mystical experience of freedom are comprehended. Berdyaev, again, gives trenchant statement in religio-mystical terms to the positive and creative meaning of freedom.[2]

> The creative act is a free and independent force, immanently inherent only in a person, a personality. Only something arising in original substance and possessing the power to increase power in the world can be true creativity. . . . Creativity . . . is an original act of personalities in the world.

Berdyaev further describes the nature of freedom:[3]

> Only the free man creates. The determinism which is so compulsively forced upon us is false because freedom of personality does exist, creatively breaking the chains of necessity. We cannot understand the creative secret of being in a passive way, in an atmosphere of obedience to the world's heavy materialism. It can be understood only actively, in the atmosphere of the creative act itself.

Such elevated motives may carry their own penalty, in the form of a loss of contact with ordinary human feeling and an unrealistic inflation of one's own self-estimate. The Grounds of Being may be only a step from the grounds of melodrama. William James remarks somewhere on the reaction of German philosophers to the idea of the transcendental ego: "at the mention of the term they act as though a balloon is about to go up." Certainly more melodrama than research has resulted from many

---

[2]*The Meaning of the Creative Act,* p. 135.
[3]Ibid., p. 155.

of the explorations with the hallucinogenic drugs in contexts which emphasize the transcendental nature of the experience. The so-called "psychedelic movement" has produced rare blooms indeed in the "hippies," "human be-ins," "psychedelic celebrations," and "psychedelic art," as well as contributing to the language such terms as "turned on," "trips," and so on. That it somehow did meet a widely felt social need for novelty of experience and perception must be acknowledged. The role of LSD-25 and related drugs in all this has been decisive, and on the face of it the drugs have led to certain social and personal novelties.

The question remains, Do these drugs affect factors in creativity in a scientifically demonstrated way? The soundest study from the measurement point of view that has come to our attention is that of McGlothlin, Cohen, and McGlothlin (1967). In their experiment, a large battery of psychological tests was given prior to a series of three LSD sessions in each of which the experimental subjects (24 male graduate students) ingested 200 mg of LSD-25, about twice as much as the quantity considered necessary to produce the usual clinical effect. Two weeks after the third LSD session, and again six months after the third session, the test battery was readministered. Control groups were utilized, one of which received 25 mg of LSD and the other 20 mg of amphetamine. Unlike most experiments with LSD, in this one subjects were not informed of the nature of the study until after they had volunteered to take part, for pay, in what was announced simply as a psychological experiment. The set and setting could be described as a secure and supportive environment, with minimal motivation, expectation, or suggestion of the sort that might dispose the subjects to expect their creativity to increase.

Under these circumstances, one would not expect very spectacular changes, and indeed only minor changes occurred. Nevertheless, for the experimental group, 17 of the 18 changes indicated by the test results were in the hypothesized direction. They were summarized as follows by the experimenters: (1) lower anxiety; (2) attitude and personality changes, primarily characterized by less egocentrism, materialism, and competitiveness, less defensiveness and aggression, and greater introspectiveness, tolerance towards others, and honesty with regard to self; (3) increased creativity; and (4) enhanced interest in and apprecia- tion of music and art. The creativity tests in the battery included four of the Guilford tests of divergent thinking abilities: Associa- tional Fluency, Alternate Uses, Plot Titles, and Hidden Figures. The changes observed, although consistent, were quite small and of little practical significance.

This careful and well-controlled study suffers from the defect of its virtues, however. In their zeal for measurement-based evi- dence, the investigators chose to use short and precisely timed tests of the sort employed in Guilford's factor analytic studies. Since factor analysis depends on standardized measurement of many variables in the same group of subjects, the factor analysts naturally prefer such short, closely timed tests to meet the practi- cal difficulties presented in gaining the cooperation of subjects for such data collection. The tests are certainly very useful, as we have seen; however, they are not the instruments of choice for observing creative problem solving in which a high-level integral act of intellect is called for. Moreover, they put a premium upon speed of response and leave no room for the incubation process or for the sort of mental state we call reverie (musing, meditation, contemplation, "brown study"). In fact, they call for precisely the sorts of behavior that we would not expect a psychedelic drug to affect to any great extent.

With these considerations in mind, experimenters at the Psy- chedelic Research Institute (now defunct) at San Francisco State College (Moger et al., 1966) took quite a different tack. As subjects of study they selected highly trained practitioners of such professions as architecture, engineering, mathematics, furniture design, physics, and so on. They required of each subject that he be presently at work upon a difficult problem in his field for which he had been unable to find a solution. In instructions to the subjects they emphasized that the psychedelic drug session in which they were to take part had as its primary aim the consider-

ation of the specific problem with which the individual was engaged in his professional work. It was strongly emphasized that
the sessions would *not* be oriented towards help with personal
problems, *not* be directed towards religious experience, *not* be
aimed at novel sensory experience, and so on. The aim of the
session was simply to consider a specific intellectual problem
while under the influence of a psychedelic drug (in this case,
LSD-25).

Twenty-two subjects took part in the experiment, each in
individual sessions, in the home of one of the experimenters. The
sessions began in mid-morning, and there was a clear understanding with the subject beforehand about the time schedule, including arrangements for dinner and for transportation back to his
own home in the evening. Every effort was made to produce an
atmosphere of psychological safety combined with intellectual
freedom in a responsible and serious search both for answers to
the problems the subjects brought and for insight into creative
mental processes under the influence of a psychedelic drug.

There are three sources of evidence for the results of this
procedure. The subjects used tape recorders, as well as pencil and
paper, to report verbally their thoughts in the course of the
sessions. Within a few days after the session, each subject wrote a
report on what had occurred, particularly in relation to the problem he was working on. Finally, a follow-up several months later
investigated the practical consequences of this effort at problem
solution.

These data provide richly detailed evidence that the experiment indeed stimulated creative processes. The interested reader
is referred to the report of the experiment (*Psychological Reports,* 1966). Excerpts from it may be found in a recent book,
LSD: The Problem-solving Psychedelic, by P. G. Stafford and B.
H. Golightly; their volume also brings together a number of
observations scattered throughout the clinical literature on LSD
that are relevant to the question of its effect on creativity. The
difficulty, of course, with such anecdotal accounts is that no
experimental controls have been introduced to ensure specificity

of the drug effects; hypnotic trance alone, for example, has been reported to facilitate creative thinking (Bowers, 1967), and no doubt intensified motivation and attention to the problem will do so as well. Nor can one be sure that the individual could not have solved the problem anyhow.

What is needed, it seems clear, is controlled experimentation of the McGlothin *et al.* variety, combined with selection of problems of a high order of challenge and complexity. Such research is not easy to do even under the most favorable circumstances of social support and financial backing, and these are lacking at present. There is also some possibility that the major psychedelic drugs may be physically dangerous (as distinct from psychologically upsetting when misused). M. M. Cohen (1967) has reported observing chromosomal damage in human blood cells caused by LSD-25, and there are other as yet inconclusive reports along the same lines.

These experiments are beset by technical difficulties, however, and they are limited too by the fact that the demonstration does not extend to cells not removed from the organism. Furthermore, chromosomal breakage is known to result from cell interaction in a test tube with such common substances as sugar, table salt, and aspirin. Recent experiments reported by the Food and Drug Administration have even implicated the popular low calorie soft drinks (for rite diets) as possibly causing chromosomal damage through the action of the artificial sweetening agents used.

It is perhaps too early to form a sound opinion of the dangers of LSD, even though it can be said without question that the drug can trigger psychosis in certain persons under certain circumstances. The fact that other drugs, such as the tranquilizers, the amphetamines, various alcohols, and the ovulation "regulators," all of which have spread in epidemic fashion during the past decade, may be much more dangerous is no argument. The problem of social control over abuse of all sorts of drugs that throw our mental and physical systems out of kilter is a paramount problem for human beings in the decade to come.

Granting this, it must be said that control of the hallucinogenic drugs by blanket prohibition is a manifestation of lack of creativity and imagination in legislators. The books are not yet closed on the question of whether the higher mental faculties may be influenced beneficially by means of chemical agents. It has been found, for example, that a number of substances, such as strychnine in small doses, picrotoxin, physostigmine (an anticholinesterase—a substance which interferes with the destruction of certain transmitter molecules in the brain), if administered before a learning experience seem to improve the rate of learning of spatial discriminations, visual discriminations for food, and avoidance responses to prevent punishment. Other substances, such as serotonin, seem to interfere with the rate of learning if they are present in increased concentrations. Many of the materials that cause alteration in learning ability share the property of causing changes in the concentration of certain substances in the brain, notably potassium and calcium. In one study, cats who received a small amount of potassium injected directly into the brain before each learning experience learned much more rapidly, while cats who received minute injections of calcium dirctly into the brain under the same conditions learned very slowly. Thus, minute alterations in the chemical composition of brain fluids, without alteration of the fundamental anatomical structure of the brain, can produce changes in rate of learning.

The implication of all this is that anatomical differences between the brains of animals of the same species may not be the sole or even main cause of differences in intellectual ability. Both amount of stimulation in the environment and variation in the activity of enzyme systems controlling chemical reactions related to nervous excitability may be just as important as anatomical structure. This area of research is one of the most exciting frontiers of behavioral science.

Chapter Fifteen

Foundations in Childhood
of Creative Experiencing

The Education of Henry Adams has something to teach us, quite apart from its presentation of a method for understanding the direction of historical forces and the somewhat gloomy forecasts to which this led. Part of it is simply the story of a boy growing up in America, in what was perhaps a happier day, and certainly in favored company. Few of us are "ticketed through" as the boy Henry was, and one can hope for no correspondence, or indeed seek one, between his education and ours. The world and the United States are moving along and daily experience is so different, in the particulars that claim ordinary attention, from anything possible in those days that began in 1838.

Yet in the real fundaments of experience, nothing changes. *The Education of Henry Adams* is dedicated to a central perplexity which disclosed itself to its author and engaged his life as he carried it to the edge. He put it in terms similar to some we have considered fundamental to the creative process: the multiplicity (to the point of meaninglessness) of the world as science reveals it, and the unity and enduringness of the sense of selfhood.

The *Education* is in a sense a parable, for it likens a life to a journey in which all the starts and stops are planned from the beginning, and the final destination assured, only to have the traveler show no interest in the itinerary. The stations were not what occupied him; he was pleased more by the passage, which permitted him to look out the window upon a variety of scenes and to reflect.

The education of Henry Adams was, he tells us, by incident and accident, through a course of mental development quite unforeseen. He gives us many vivid details of shaping events and circumstances. Two of these in particular have stayed in my own mind, so clearly do they catch important "educational" moments.

The first of these incidents has to do with that big event in a boy's life, being made to go to school when he would much rather be out playing. In Henry Adams's case, the day came while his family was visiting his grandfather, then President of the United States.

All the more singular it seemed afterwards to him that his first serious contact with the President should have been a struggle of will, in which the old man almost necessarily defeated the boy, but instead of leaving, as usual in such defeats, a lifelong sting, left rather an impression of as fair treatment as could be expected from a natural enemy. The boy met seldom with such restraint. He could not have been more than six years old at the time— seven at the utmost—and his mother had taken him to Quincy for a long stay with the President during the summer. What became of the rest of the family he quite forgot; but he distinctly remembered standing at the house door one summer morning in a passionate outburst of rebellion against going to school. Naturally his mother was the immediate victim of his rage; that is what mothers are for, and boys also; but in this case the boy had his mother at unfair disadvantage, for she was a guest, and had no means of enforcing obedience. Henry showed a certain tactical ability by refusing to start, and he met all efforts at compulsion by successful, though too vehement, protest. He was in fair way to win, and was holding his own, with sufficient energy, at the bottom of the long staircase which led up to the door of the President's library, when the door opened, and the old man slowly came down. Putting on his hat, he took the boy's hand without a word, and walked with him, paralyzed by awe, up the road to the town. After the first moments of consternation at this interference in a domestic dispute, the boy reflected that an old gentleman close on eighty would never trouble himself to walk near a mile on a hot summer morning over a shadeless road to take a boy to school, and that it would be strange if a lad imbued with the passion of freedom could not find a corner to dodge around, somewhere before reaching the school door. Then and always, the boy insisted that this reasoning justified his apparent submission; but the old man did not stop, and the boy saw all his strategical points turned, one after another, until he found himself seated inside the school. . . . Not till then did the President release his hand and depart.

The point was that this act, contrary to the inalienable rights of boys, and nullifying the social compact, ought to have made him dislike his grandfather for life. He could not recall that it had this effect for a moment. With a certain maturity of mind, the child must have recognized that the President, though a tool of tyranny, had done his disreputable work with a certain intelligence. He had shown no temper, no irritation, no personal feeling and had made no display of force. Above all, he had held his tongue. During their long walk he had said nothing; he had uttered no syllable of revolting cant about the duty of obedience and the wickedness of resistance to law; he had shown no concern in the matter. . . . For this forbearance (the boy) felt instinctive respect.[1]

The second incident taught another lesson that one is lucky if one learns:

One of the commonest boy-games of winter, inherited directly from the eighteenth century, was a game of war on Boston Common . . . in practise, a battle of the Latin School against all comers. Whenever, on a half-holiday, the weather was soft enough to soften the snow, the Common was apt to be the scene of a fight, which began in daylight with the Latin School in force, rushing their opponents down to Tremont Street, and which generally ended at dark by the Latin School dwindling in numbers and disappearing.

One afternoon the fight had been long and exhausting. The boy Henry, following, as his habit was, his bigger brother Charles, had taken part in the battle, and had felt his courage much depressed by seeing one of his trustiest leaders, Henry Higginson—"Bully Hig," his school name—struck by a stone over the eye, and led off the field bleeding in rather a ghastly manner. As night came on, the Latin School was steadily forced back to the Beacon Street Mall where they could retreat no further without disbanding, and by that time only a small band was left, headed by two heroes, Savage and Marvin. A dark mass of figures could be seen below, making ready for the last rush, and rumor said that a swarm of blackguards from the slums, led by a grisly terror called Conky Daniels, with a club and a hideous reputation, was going to put an end to the Beacon Street cowards forever. Henry wanted to run away with the others, but his brother was too big to run away, so they stood still and waited immolation. The dark mass set up a shout, and rushed forward. The Beacon Street boys turned and fled up the steps, except Savage and Marvin and the few champions who would not run. The terrible Conky Daniels swaggered up, stopped a moment with his bodyguard to swear a few oaths at Marvin, and then swept on and chased the flyers, leaving the few boys untouched who stood their ground . . . but the boy Henry had passed through as much terror as though he were Turenne or Henry IV, and ten or twelve years afterwards when these same boys were fighting and falling on all the battlefields of Virginia and Maryland he wondered whether their education on Boston Common had taught Savage and Marvin how to die.[2]

These two episodes in the education of Henry Adams are slight enough as events: a boy of six being taken to school against his will, and a boy of eleven standing his ground in a snowball fight. Yet they are primary educational experiences, which no amount of design by educators could have arranged; such things happen only of themselves. And they are not only primary, but fundamental: acceptance without rancor of the taming of the will, and learning something of how to die. Henry Adams was fortunate in his companions and exemplars.

Education as Henry Adams wrote of it deals with the integration of fundamental and primary experiences in the development of the self. Creativity is one possible outcome of education in this sense of the term. To look further at the educational conditions that favor the development of creativity in a person, let us consider the experiential fundaments of the self, conceived as encounters with universal forces provided by the nature of the world, of individual human life, and of culture.

These fundaments are given, I believe, in our own physical and psychical structure and in the furniture and the motion picture of the firmament, which itself has generated both the viewer and the viewed, the eye that looks and the interior and exterior realities that are reflected and that are changed in the perceiving. Though the mind may balk at the idea, cosmological reconstruction of the history of the physical universe tells us that at some point the universe itself generated the structure with which it could view itself. In a sense, it opened an eye upon itself, the prototype of the reflective act.

The rudiments of consciousness proceed from the function of the eye itself in discrimination of outside and inside, opening and shutting, letting in light or excluding it. Whether a thing moves or does not move is of primitive importance, and in lower forms this is expressed simply as reaction to the presence or absence of light.

The human infant, upon opening his eyes, in those first days of establishing place and person, will fixate upon the eyes of the mother, there to find assurance of stability and "looking after" in the face of the unfamiliar. Not to be able to establish an outside is the condition of selflessness, to be taken in both its negative and positive possibilities. "The idiot greens the meadow with his eyes" is a poetic statement, by Allen Tate, of the failure in this fundamental discrimination, although it suggests also a potentiality in this lack of ability to discriminate outer from inner.

The sensory nonvisual world comes to help, of course. There is wet and dry, and hot and cold, and up and down, and pressure ("it hurts") and nonpressure. Even going and staying are not entirely visual. "There goes the BM" or "here it comes" or, much later, "here I come" or "here I go" are rudimentary kinesthetic discriminations of self and the world. They may later need words to go with them; and words, through the importance they take on because of their efficiency in getting us life-sustaining information, are a weighty part of our equipment. Yet the primitive kinesthetically experienced goings and comings may not only precede the verbal developmentally but, with the purely visual, may come to occupy permanently the interstices of the conceptual framework of mind. They remain there, effective though unnoticed and largely unverbalizable. To restore them to attention is surely one of the functions of the arts of sculpture, architecture, and painting.

The baby, then, notices mostly whether things are here or there, moving or still, outside or inside, wet or dry, warm or cold, pleasing or displeasing, serving or disserving, producible by action of the self or simply autonomous or the result of chance.

Perhaps the chief internal structures in these rudimentary analogues of the psychic basis of reflection, repression, and production are the orifices of the body and its integument—boundaries and portals. The production of self-initiated effects, especially in their developing reciprocal relationship with autonomous external forces, and especially also as they involve objective mastery and an internal sense or feeling of competence, serves to define the self in terms of process and structure *as reflected.* There is more to this than simple competence, however; there is fitness, or a sort of symbolic aptness or equivalence, between the self-initiated act and the *delighting* effect, which in turn serves as a fundament of ego and a motive towards creation of effects at a much later stage of development.

After these early discriminations come others which emphasize more the content and process of the firmament. Fundamental to process are rhythms: periodicities such as the gross ones of night and day and the turning of the seasons, or the more internally signaled ones of the beating of the heart or the taking in and letting out of breath. These periodicities are reinforced by the social practices that arrange themselves around physical rhythms: habitual times for taking meals, for example, or, at a more complex and symbolic level, the observation of holidays with their freight of religious meaning.

Sun and moon, stars, the wind, rocks, flowers, water, fire—these give us the colored and moving, or uncolored and stationary, world. In the childhood of philosophy, earth and fire and air and water were thought the stuff of life, and they are the universal early experiences of children. The moon is said to be the eye of night, and the sun the warming yet sometimes fierce eye of day. Not to look at the sun directly is one of the earliest adaptations, and indeed may be the prototype of the act of repression.

The seasons in their turning go sometimes in simple doubles, sometimes in double doubles; like hot and cold, we have summer and winter, and like our bodily wets and drys we have the rains and the dry spells. The moon, unlike the sun, changes shape and appears at what may seem whimsy of position and time—the moon is fickle—the moon also is definer of month, and of menses, and of mind (*mens, mentis*), and of mensuration. The eggs of females go by the moon and so do the tides, and some even think that madness or lunacy does. The moon gives us numbers to go by: 28, 14, multiples of 2 and 4 and 7. Through the sun and the moon and the seasons we learn of the wheel—gyres—the turning around and around of the great orbs. Gyration is the most forcible of the periodicities that the universe shows us in showing its face to us.

Facedness itself is one of the fundamentals of structure out of which many processes grow. We face forward in time, and we look ahead in space. What we may yet experience lies ahead of us. How we see ourselves in a mirror tells us of ourselves. Other faces too can mirror us. We may use our face to mask ourselves as well as to express or assert—and unused at all it seems to *be* ourselves.

Very early in life we learn of growth. There are bigger ones of the same shape, and we may even see photos that show they were once small. We can see ourselves growing. Near this realization comes also the realization of death—"What would happen if I became bigger and bigger and bigger?" or "Older and older and older?" And when other living beings are seen to die, the realization, the impossible realization, begins to dawn.

For the central fact of fate for everyone is death, and the ego marshals all its resources to accommodate itself to this fact. Culture is replete with the most elegant of symbolic constructions aimed at denying the finality of death. Christianity and Buddhism, while they are at opposite poles in their interpretation of the sources and governance of the cosmos, are identical in the mission assigned their archetypal personage: both Christ and the Buddha are to conquer death. The Judaic-Christian monotheistic account of the Creation, the Fall, and the Redemption is a story of God the Father's enmity towards man, God the Son's love and pity for him, and God the Holy Spirit's gift of grace; the Father establishes the law from of old, and punishes; the Son dies for all, and so redeems; the Holy Spirit comes with a saving gift, something free, and so blesses. A well-rounded tale, whether "true" or not. Some of the greatest minds of Western culture have been at pains to elaborate the metaphysics and theology of this account of the universe and man's fate, and in many cases the story has used elements of pre-Christian myths from Greece and the Middle East to establish the character of the personages of the drama. The study of myth and symbol is one of the most fascinating branches of the psychology of the ego, and it tells us over and over again that the questions of children about their origins and their fate are original religion and poetry.

The end of innocence and the beginning of experience (to use again the terms of William Blake) has as point of passage the recognition that one is fated. Death is not all of fate, of course; being a woman or a man, with all that the differentiation of sexual function entails, is one of the most powerful aspects of fate, and behind it lies the fact of permanent division of the two generative principles. Plato in *The Symposium* has given us a most beautiful statement of various human thoughts on the subject of love, and one of the most striking of these is the theory he puts into the mouth of Aristophanes: that male and female were once one but in time beyond memory were divided into two parts that continually seek one another. Herman Melville expressed this thought in a poem, which emphasizes that this aspect of fate may be a bitter one:

> What cosmic jest or anarch blunder
> The human integral clove asunder
> And shied the fractions through life's gate?

And such the dicing of blind fate
Few matching halves here meet and mate.

Changes are rung on this theme in all the love stories and the love lyrics of the world, and a nostalgia for the condition of unseparatedness must be counted among the most primitive of feelings, a response to the counterpart of death in human fate.

There are many common but less universal aspects of individual fate that enter into consciousness at nearly the same time in the child's development (differences from others in race, strength, health, beauty, status, and so on). The general point is that the recognition of the fact that fate has things in store for one, and that the individual has no choice in the matter, is significant in ego formation; this marks the end of innocence and the beginning of the development of "persona."

I believe that it is at this point that a decisive bifurcation may occur, one psychic path leading to a way of being that remains open to experience and the other leading to a personal adjustment that is "normal" but that is achieved at the cost of repression of the spontaneity and wonder of childhood. The person who is open to experience does not separate himself from the process of life by repression but rather gives himself over to the life processes within him. Because the childhood experiences are thus retained in consciousness and integrated into the personality, "regression in the service of the ego," as the psychoanalytic theorist Ernst Kris has interpreted the role of more "primitive" modes of thinking in creativity, is in fact not necessary; rather, a progression has occurred that keeps the best of innocence while moving ahead to the command and control that experience brings. I have elsewhere described creative architects whom we studied in our researches as "practical transcendentalists," and this phrase I think captures something of what I have been trying here to elucidate in terms of ego development. One might also say that in creativity we have a love marriage of innocence and experience, thus implying that they need not be separated. Or, to put it another way, the creative individual retains his innocence in the face of fate. I am reminded of a passage from the great Indian poet Rabindranath Tagore, who wrote of children:

> They build their houses with sand, and they play with empty shells. With withered leaves they weave their boats and smilingly float them on the vast deep. Children have their play on the seashore of worlds. They know not how to swim, they know not how to cast nets. Pearl-fishers dive for pearls, merchants sail in their ships, while children gather pebbles and scatter them again. They seek not for hidden treasures, they know not how to cast nets.

Yet children, we hope, will grow up; the question is, can we create such conditions of life and education that they grow up "innocent in the face of fate," that is to say, genuinely integrated and without loss of the ability to function creatively.

Chapter Sixteen

Cycles of Innocence and Experience

Something close to what William Blake meant by "innocence" as contrasted with "experience" is signified by the psychological term "prelogical thought." Prelogical thought is relatively free of abstraction and of logical structure, much as one might suppose the thought of a very young child to be. Primitive peoples are also said to experience prelogically; the whole of what is subsumed under the term "magical thinking," including animistic interpretations of events in the physical world, irrational beliefs and taboos surrounding sexuality, and the invocation of gods, demons, and witches as directly effective in the affairs of men, can be considered as prelogical. In certain types of functional psychosis, as well as in organic brain damage, there is said to be a regression to such modes of thought, with primitivization and concretizing of perception and radical reduction in the ability to classify and to generalize.

Such similarity as does exist seems to derive from the pervasiveness of symbolization in the work of artists that bears a resemblance to early nonverbal symbolic processes in the infant. But this lumping together of the experience of children, primitives, psychotics, and the organically brain-damaged seems to me to do violence to the quality of experience in children. It is true enough that in early infancy the child has very little capacity to make discriminations, and hence to establish classifications based upon comparison. His world is made up of what the poet W. H. Auden has called "large and noisy feeling-states," and in his early days the infant knows at best only such differences as we noted earlier: wet and dry, moving and still, hot and cold, full and empty, inside and outside, self and others; and even these discriminations may be uncertain and not at all surely founded. But the experience of a healthy infant is the experience of an organism whose psychological integrity is undamaged and whose potentialities are vast. Surely the quality of such experiencing is different in kind from that of an organism of restricted potential or damaged function. Poets and mystics too have sometimes been thrown into this same bin by psychoanalytic theorists, but I shall leave that absurdity aside for the moment and return to it later.

One crucial difference between children and damaged adults is in the development and exercise of ethical judgment and responsibility. The evolution of the very early and basic discriminations into a structure which arrives finally at "the making up of mind" in the sense of ethical discriminations or judgments of the value of actions in terms of good or bad has been beautifully presented in symbolic form in the first chapter of James Joyce's novel, *A Portrait of the Artist as a Young Man*. The protagonist, a boy who is, at the end of this process, trying to make up his mind whether there are circumstances in which it is all right or even required to "peach on a chap," has passed from childish innocence to a certain sort of "experience," the experience now being freighted with logical argument and being derived from the teaching of his particular form of society concerning good and evil. We might say that his experience was now no longer prelogical; in the words of the penny catechism, he had "attained the use of reason." In those days "the use of reason" was considered to arrive at about age six, at about the same time that one started to go to school.

In our own day, of course, we know that the use of reason does not arrive all of a sudden, but that with growing structuration of the world perceptually and with the acquisition of habits of thought the capacity to reason inferentially is growing apace. Thus, if childhood experience can ever be said to be prelogical, it should be said to be *relatively* prelogical.

If you will accept with me then that prelogicality in children is a relative matter and a question of degree and quality of perceptual structure rather than an absence of it, perhaps postlogicality by the same token can be given a useful meaning. The intervening condition is simply that of the sensible man, with firmly established concepts, easy and effective ability to attend and remember, an integrated set of values, a flexible repression mechanism which allows him to be fully conscious of most of his personal experience yet capable of excluding from consciousness thoughts or feelings that might prove maladaptive, and, as a result of these attributes, good practical judgment in adapting himself to social reality and in getting on in life. Such a person may be logical and sensible without particular strain, yet not be characterized by certain other qualities that either go beyond logic or seem to exist apart from it, such as mysticism, visionary wisdom, and creativity in art and science. Rationality, logic, reason—all those good things by which we might hope the world's affairs could be run—often seem to be the enemies of poetic imagination. The philosopher Jacques Maritain, indeed, sees as one of the principal steps in the evolution of modern art, especially poetry and painting, "liberation from and transformation of . . . rational language." He writes, in *Creative Intuition in Art and Poetry*:

> Rational language is not cut out to express the singular, it is burdened with social and utilitarian connotations, ready-made associations, and worn-out meanings, it is invaded by the inevitable insipidity which results from habit. So it does not only interfere with poetry, it perpetually sidetracks it and makes poetry say something other than what poetry wants to say. The same observation can be made with regard to that intelligible

discursus—organizing together, according to the accustomed patterns of the pleasure of the eyes or the ears, the movements of the design or the sounds of the melody—which is the rational language of painting and music. Why should we be surprised by the fact that modern artists struggle to free themselves from rational language and its logical laws? Never did they pay more attention to words, never did they attach greater importance to words: but (they do so) in order to transfigure them, and to get clear of the language of discursive reason. . . . Be it a poem or a painting, the work speaks: it speaks no longer in terms of logical reason.

But this is "reason as prison" of which Maritain speaks, bonds the creative artist seeks to break. Aristotle's "creative reason" is another matter entirely, and even the modern artist's effort at escaping the limitations of the consensus is in the service finally of reason in this sense of a free, creating generative principle. We have been impressed, in seeking to relate the creative writer's work to his life, with the force of a special intellectual motive: the cosmological motive, a strong desire to create a private cosmos of meaning through work which is grounded in the individual artist's unique being.

Mysticism has characteristically served a practical aim: the attainment of a feeling of rapport or actual identity with a transcendent power or a form of being higher and more subtle than ordinary sensibility can reach. In doing so, it does not eschew the use of ordinary reason in the development of the prologue to the mystical act itself; a comprehensive though sometimes unrecognized rational structure is basic as a point of departure for the most advanced and highly developed forms of mysticism, such as we see in Plotinus and in Eckhart. The church has traditionally been wary of its mystics, though tolerant of them so long as they did not prove dangerous to themselves or to the business of the day. This is eminently consistent with Roman Catholic theology, with its emphasis upon the union of the divine and the human in the organic body of the church. Disease and malformations are to be expected in the natural course of events in the development of the human form, and the thing to do is watch them and take measures against them only if they become a persistent sore point or an actual danger to the organism. Mysticism in these terms is best understood as an altered state of consciousness, which can be expected to occur regularly though infrequently in the body of the church and it is indeed rather interesting and at times salutary and valuable, even though it is psychically a rarefied condition which—unless surrounded by the safeguards of doctrine, dogma, ethical practice, and approved ritual and symbol—may become aberrant.

Disciplined mysticism is in this sense analogous to the creative use of material from the personal and collective unconscious; what the church refers to as "spiritualism and related errors" is akin to exploring the collective unconscious without bringing to bear upon the mass of perceptions and potentialities there the faculties of attention, discrimination, judgment, and the responsibility for shaping the nascent forms for entry into consciousness.

As for visionary wisdom, I am thinking here of that form of wisdom so deeply intuitive that it seems to pass beyond words, concepts, and practical judgment into an area of empathic understanding that is completely nonverbal. The wisdom of the Zen master or the Yoga is said to be of this kind, and perhaps as a goal of development it is more typically Eastern than Western. If prelogical experience is said to consist of the not yet conceptualizable, or the relatively unverbalizable, then postlogical experience might be said to be fully conscious and attentive inner silence. What this silence implies is that all the words in the world will not do. As P. W. Bridgman has argued in his monograph. *The Nature of Physical Reality,* it is highly probable that there are large stretches of individual experience for which there has been no need as yet to develop words and concepts, and still other stretches of experience which are inexpressible conceptually. They are therefore more difficult to bring to conscious attention, since we are so habituated to language as the most appropriate adaptive mechanism. The extension of consciousness through training in attention to the nonverbal has been a goal not only of the Eastern philosophies but of certain esoteric Christian communities as well. One of the most ancient and persistent of religious ideas is that through constant and honest attention to all the acts of one's life one can escape the cycle of birth and death; the Buddha at his death is said to have had present in his consciousness the totality not only of his final incarnation but of all the incarnations through which he had passed. The great act of attention is all-inclusive; the more of life that is experienced and remembered and brought to bear upon the present moment in living expression, the higher is the grade of wisdom.

Psychoanalysis partakes in this religious tradition in its application to individual psychotherapy of the notion of honest and unremitting attention to all the details of past and present which are potentially accessible to consciousness. The "repetition compulsion" is the psychoanalytic analogue to imprisonment in the cycle of death and rebirth; the neurotic "dies" to no avail, he runs his compulsive course to his particular form of repeatable ruin without ever knowing what is happening. "Unhappy he who dies to himself unknown," goes an old Latin proverb. Only the unrepressed and undefended life can lead to true "death," so that nothing need be repeated.

Creative individuals come in all ages and sizes, I believe, but visionary wisdom does seem to require a preliminary finely articulated and complex intellectual structure as well as deep intuition and empathy. So too do certain kinds of creativity, and I think it important to advance a number of points which may help in understanding the nature of creative activity in childhood. It is almost a commonplace by now that children very often have a kind of spontaneity, freedom, imagination, and creativeness that adults all too often lack. Many educators, as we have seen, have been led to suspect that the school system itself may somehow be destroying the precious spark of creativity in youngsters by producing conformity pressures, by over-emphasizing routine and drill, and perhaps even by unwise and rigid discipline. The question is not quite that simple, however, and I think we should look at it more closely.

First of all, we must note the fact that a considerable amount of training and discipline is necessary for most sorts, if not indeed all sorts, of work that can reach a high level of creativeness. This certainly is true of the outstanding products of our culture, whether we think of musical compositions, painting and sculpture, problem solving and theory construction in mathematics and the sciences, architecture, or such performances as ballet dancing and operatic singing. Long years of discipline, training, and devotion are necessary. Moreover, such work is generally directed towards an audience capable of understanding and receiving or appreciating the work, while children's inventiveness and spontaneous creativity do not have these characteristics, either in demand or in intention. In brief, a certain amount of maturation of the talent, and discipline in its exercise, must precede its full expression. Since this also *takes time*, the complex creative act can be expected to occur only rarely in childhood, or before maturation has taken place.

Yet these considerations do not really touch upon the observation that many children but relatively few adults seem to be spontaneously imaginative and free in expression. Most adults rarely play or sing or paint or make up new words or expressions; the Muses seem to prefer children. The question is this: Does the loss of potential for creative expression occur as a consequnce of some organic law, or is it that we *learn* to inhibit creativity in ourselves? The question has the greatest importance for education and for society as a whole, since we shall need all of the potential creativity of human beings if we are to solve the problems now confronting us as a species.

To seek an answer to this question, let us return to a consideration of the history of development of perceptual structure through comparison and classification. The structures that develop are selective largely in terms of survival value to the individual organism. The essential function of conceptualization and of the establishment of perceptual habits is to increase the ability to discern regularities so that destructive contingencies may be foreseen and avoided and constructive possibilities entertained.

In other words, in the evolution of life, what was most necessary for the organism was that events be predicted so that self-preservative action could be made ready. The mechanism for achieving such an ability to predict is classification, or the perception of similarity and repetition. The conceptualizing intellect therefore seeks out in every situation that which is already familiar, so that the principle "like produces like" may be applied. The most abstract and far-reaching extension of this essential principle is embodied in the structure of science, which applies rigorous method to avoid error of observation and inference, but which does not depart essentially from pristine common sense in its goal, which is to discern repetition.

This heavy dependence upon repetition is confronted by the fact that life itself is continually producing novelty. Determinative factors can often be seen only in retrospect. The creative intellect is therefore always ready to abandon classifications known from the past and to acknowledge in its strongest form the proposition that life, including one's individual life, is pregnant with unheard-of possibilities and may be the vehicle for transformations without precedent. When such a possibility is acknowledged, the coercive power of all known systems of classification and the predictive value of regularities based upon a history of repetition may be set aside in favor of an openness to the forces of life pressing for novel expression, both in one's individual existence and through it as a vehicle for the creation of an unforeseeable future.

What this presents us with, then, is the paradox of discipline and freedom, a paradox that shows itself under many names: habit and flexibility, order and disorder, integration and diffusion. The task we face is to avoid sacrificing one possibility to the other. We must be able to use discipline to gain greater freedom, take on habits in order to increase our flexibility, permit disorder in the interests of an emerging higher order, tolerate diffusion, and even occasionally invite it, in order to achieve a more complex integration. The passage from childhood to adulthood is fraught with the danger of one-sidedness in either direction, and every parent or teacher faces the problem in helping children to realize their creative potential to the fullest. Even chancellors of universities are not immune, and they especially have their hands full if their student bodies are unusually creative and full of promise for the future. Sigmund Freud in one of his lighter though still pessimistic moments once wrote: "There are three activities on behalf of others which one may be sure will not be rewarded with the gratitude of those who benefit from them: governing a state, raising a family, and conducting a psychoanalysis."

There is, by the way, another way of formulating the problem of inhibition of creativity. This is in terms of Freud's theory of the unconscious. Many writers and artists have in fact assigned to their own unconscious mental life a crucial role in their creativity, seeing it as the source of inspiration. Psychoanalysis of course seeks to broaden the sphere of influence of consciousness by intervention in the unconscious, with the goals both of freeing unconscious contents and freeing also the psychic energy being used uneconomically in the neurosis to keep ideational representations of tabooed and repressed drives "bound" in the unconscious.

I should like to suggest that it is quite possible that repressions instituted in the child both in the family circle and in the educational system may result not simply in the development of an inhibiting unconscious in the Freudian sense, but in the actual restriction of a natural tendency in children towards play, music, drawing and painting, and many forms of nonverbal sensory grasping and symbolizations. And I think also that this need not be a matter of repression, but simply of denial of opportunity for expression. The school world is so much a world of words and books and depends heavily upon—and I mean this in two senses—classes; but the natural world to which the child has, before school, been relating himself is much more sensorially variegated and much less shepherding. If verbally docile sheep result, we should not be surprised.

Let me say all this once again, more briefly and in a different way. In the creative process there is an incessant dialectic and an essential tension between two seemingly opposed dispositional tendencies: the tendency towards structuring and integration and the tendency towards disruption of structure and diffusion and energy and attention. The marks of integration are: (1) differentiation and discrimination; (2) classification in the interest of prediction (which would include broadly all sorts of communions, amalgamations, and incorporations for the sake of increasing power); and (3) establishment of perceptual constancies, or selective perceptual adaptations (taking of habits, establishment of sovereignties).

When differentiation has occurred, the original walls now enclose more than one chamber. In human beings, the chambers are numbered in the billions, and the human brain is the most elegant of mansions. Differentiation, together with adaptative dispositional tendencies that make discrimination possible, permits the focusing of energy at a single point; in a sense, the organism becomes able to face things, to attend. Moreover, and this we usually do not think of, differentiation means that individual death is in the offing; the rule is that whatever grows must die. The very act of establishing a class brings a sort of death to all the unique attributes of the objects classified, although at the same time it gives new power because it is a step towards regularity and law. In human relationship, itself a form of classification, by making common cause we gain strength individually from the new unit and bring a new form of being into existence, though at the cost of some unassimilable unique attributes of each individual.

This fact of existence leads to one of the basic paradoxes of human development: The more fully developed and finely articulated we become, the less the *possibility for alternative integration*. But one of the amazing features of the human brain is that it permits the possible to survive alongside the actualized; whatever is potential in mind is not damaged by not being actualized, even though in the individual life there may not be time enough for a return to bypassed possibilities.

The interesting fact for creativity about conditions that bring about diffusion is that very often they restore a certain naïveté of perception. One of the poets who served as a subject in my study of creative writers was at that time in his early fifties and was the father of three young children, the products of a late and very happy marriage. He felt that he had been unexpectedly blessed, that he had been "lucky" after a turbulent and changeful youth and early middle age. Yet as he told me of this good fortune and of his pleasure in his home and family, he added musingly, half to himself, "I wonder whether I'll ever write anything really new from now on. I don't think I could ever throw myself away again."

What this man meant by "throwing himself away" is what in this context we mean by permitting diffusion to occur in the service of a need for an enrichment of conscious experience—a need felt with such intensity that the individual is willing to "die unto himself," that is, to permit an achieved adaptation or state of relative equilibrium to perish. And there are no guarantees that something better will thereby be arrived at. Looking backwards from the end point of the creative process, we are inclined to say, "Ah, yes, it had to be so; the chance had to be taken; the chalice could not be passed; the agony was necessary for the redemption and the resurrection." But facing forward in time we see only risk and difficulty, and if we have not the courage to endure diffusion ("suffer death") we cannot achieve the new and more inclusive integration ("gain the light"). The expansion of consciousness requires the temporary abandonment of certain ego structures, at least the crustier outside ones which are farthest from the core of what William James called "the transcendental ego" (which I conceive of as "inside" or "within" in the same sense in which Christ spoke of the kingdom of God as "within").

The appositeness to psychology of these religious metaphors and personifications (as well as the use I have made of them in this attempt at a naturalistic account of certain aspects of the creative process) is an interesting fact in itself. There need not be any fundamental oppositions between science, art, and religion; all are "mind at work," though each assumes a different posture. A link perhaps is provided by a common Latin root: *pono, ponere, posui, positus.* Postulate, posture, pose, posit, position: what each signifies is a form of local integration. And human intellection as a whole, we may guess, is itself only a partial integration. Science, art, and religion may then be understood as differentiated and valid expressions of possibilities actualized in our local form of mind.

This emphasis upon shifting patterns of diffusion and integration gives us a somewhat restless view of the creative process if we omit enduring attention. And in the individual life, after all, there is something good to be said for knowing when to take in sail. Psychological growth too has its pathological aspect, and there is a cancerous kind of ego expansion which occurs when no bounds to individuality are recognized. One of the characteristics of normal tissue is that it contains intrinsic and inherent restraints upon its own growth. Surely something of the same sort exists in normal psychological development. To each of us is given a span of attention and a span of years, and both are brief but wondrous. The enduringness of attention through the cycles of change enables us to complete the whole.

Appendix

Ideas for Social and Economic Innovation in Ireland

An interesting byproduct of the assessment study of innovators in business management in Ireland is the actual set of ideas generated by the managers in response to some of the assessment tests and situations. In Chapter 8 we saw what sorts of personal and intellectual traits characterized the most outstandingly original managers. What of their ideas? What had these individuals, who had distinguished themselves by a fresh approach to their own business enterprises, to contribute when asked to address themselves to the general question, "What new things (social institutions, customs, products, services, kinds of people and skills), are needed in Ireland?"

The methods used to obtain their answers to this question were a combination of written "tests," brainstorming, and group discussion. We shall present a sampling of results of the test approach first, then go on to the fruits of group discussion and brainstorming.

THE CONSEQUENCES FOR IRELAND TEST

The format used by Wilson and Guilford (1953) in the Consequences test (and earlier by Bennett in his Test for Productive Thinking) was modified in this case to make most of the test items relevant to Ireland rather than to the world at large. Some of the standard Consequences items were retained, however, in order that level of originality on non-Irish consequences could be compared with originality in responding to Irish problems; this was done in the expectation that discrepancies of performance on the two kinds of items might be related to religious philosophy, an expectation that proved unfounded so far as we have been able to discover.

The Consequences for Ireland problems and some characteristic responses gleaned from the records of the more highly innovative managers were as follows:

The "Consequences" Test

PROBLEM 1

As a result of a remarkable scientific breakthrough by an Irish physicist, Ireland alone of all countries in the world has at her disposal virtually unlimited supplies of nuclear energy at little cost. What could be the consequences?

> A gradual but cumulative development of industry which would transform the economy. Ireland would rapidly become a powerful economic force.
>
> A gradual development of agriculture through heating of soil and provision of food in processed form for animals.
>
> Control eventually of weather through ability to create or retard precipitation.
>
> Development of scientific education to allow greater use of the atomic resources.
>
> Scientific attainment would help tear down the "Green Curtain."

Ireland would become a World Wide Retirement Centre, and we'd still have all the greenery we are famous for.

Destruction of Irish culture with excessive foreign capital and emphasis on material wealth.

PROBLEM 2

Genetic changes produced by increased nuclear radiation prove to be sex-linked for intelligence alone, and it is specifically the intelligence of women that will undergo an increase in magnitude. In Ireland, what would be the consequences?

The gradual elimination of male dominance in decision taking, in business, in government.

Emphasis on physical beauty by women, to cover their greater IQ.

Disillusion with intelligence as an indication of general ability.

Gradual female take-over of the initiative in partner selection for marriage.

Fall in population.

Homes would be better planned and better organized and equipped.

Children would get better home education.

Unlikely to affect traditional relationships, e.g., women not likely to become leaders in home with even a 15 percent increase in intelligence. Tradition and religion would discourage woman as leader.

Change in educational patterns as more women take graduate courses.

Incursion of women into Government.

PROBLEM 3

The government makes a firm decision to abandon the teaching of Irish in the schools and to replace it with the most up-to-date methods of teaching mathematics and the natural and physical sciences. What would be the consequences?

Tremendous agitation.

At long last the inherent intelligence present in every Irishman's make-up would see some of the daylight.

Higher productivity—there is no productivity benefit in the teaching of Irish.

A retarding of ability to communicate through elimination of the mental qualities which come from a second language.

The likely loss of office by the Government.

The government in question would be remembered in history as the most enlightened since we achieved independence.

There might be a dilution of literary achievement in the country.

Possibility of the Irish culture and Irish personality disappearing in a comparatively short period, as these have evolved over generations during which Irish was at least to some extent studied and spoken.

In a little time the language revival would become a real issue and the language truly would be revived.

Providing that the teaching methods relating to the new subjects were not too narrow there would exist for the first time a good chance of saving the very excellent literature and culture of old Irish from utter extinction.

PROBLEM 4

Because of a sudden increase in attractive investment opportunities elsewhere, all foreign industry suddenly decides to pull out of Ireland. What would be the consequences?

If this were to happen there would be catastrophe because so much industry has foreign investment.

Grave unemployment, redistribution of remaining capital. Excessively social in character, steps inadequate.

Living standards drop to extremely low level.

Collapse of the economy as we know it now with a very severe balance of payment crisis.

Unemployment.

Emigration.

Productive foreign investment has been desirable but some is not, e.g., grip of foreign investment on retail outlets (chain stores, etc.) would be broken. One would hope that the challenge would bring out the idealism which can always be drawn on when a country is really up against it.

But there would be employment, emigration and hardship for many years followed by a gradual return to prosperity. We would be far better off however in the long run. This would be a national challenge with adversity and patriotism as the energisers. The country would, at this stage, be fully capable of getting on without foreign industry.

Turn the empty factories into Vast Hen Houses, Pip Houses, Cattle Rearing Lands. Revert to our old system of emigration. Turn factories into dance halls.

Loss of technological "know how" with long term consequences (adverse).

PROBLEM 5

The Catholic Church revises its teachings on marriage in many respects, with the result that mixed marriages are encouraged, divorce for reason of serious personal incompatibility becomes acceptable, and chemical means of birth control are permitted. What would be the consequences for Ireland?

Such reversal unsettles Catholicism so dramatically that Ireland ceases to be Christian country.

Rapprochement with Northern Ireland would become more attainable.

Less prejudice without and within country.

Many many happier marriages, where the present strain of safeperiod is intolerable.

More juvenile sex.

So long as the relaxations mentioned were introduced sensibly and without hysteria or without pushing the limits too far the people of Ireland would mature greatly in as short a time as 10 years.

Divergent line by Irish Hierarchy from Rome.

Peace of Mind with some Birth Control.

Men would be more promiscuous. Men would not be as secure or as trusting.

Better and less parochial outlook on rest of world.

PROBLEM 6

Universal free education through to the post-graduate University level or its equivalent in all fields is made widely available in Ireland to both men and women. What would be the consequences?

Large scale emigration. Too much competition for available opportunities.

Vast frustration, dissatisfaction, unrest, strikes, inflation, economic collapse.

An explosive growth in numbers attending universities.

Improvement in national productivity because of greater investment in education.

Probably, if properly handled, a great social revolution in thinking and attitudes of the "working and middle classes" due to increased opportunities for their children in a more socially enlightened society.

The social upset would be enormous as suddenly many of our professional people would come from an unusual source.

More doctors, dentists and other professionals. Great emigration among these professionals.

Expansion of sciences, business administration and similar faculties more than traditional areas.

Ultimately the only real answer for Ireland.

More intelligent use of leisure. More reading, theatre, books, plays.

A much better governing class which now suffers badly from lack of education in key local and national government posts.

PROBLEM 7

All alcohol is effectively prohibited in Ireland. What would be the consequences?

Hard to visualise the impossible.

Vast increase in legitimate and illegitimate births; you've got to do something in the country in the evening!

Ridicule in the eyes of the world.

Punitive dictatorship. Secret Police. Concentration camps. Business collapse on a large scale with unemployment.

Increase in suicide rate.

More foreign travel for the satisfaction of thirst.

Grave lowering of the standard of conversation.

Collapse (me for a start).

Day Excursion fares at low rates to Great Britain.

A serious increase in alcoholism.

More mental illness.

Rightly so. — I mean, Revolution.

Drug-taking increase.

Sickness increase.

Life would be sadder, quieter, less civilised.

PROBLEM 8

The Six-County border is removed and Ireland becomes a political unity. What would be the consequences for Ireland?

Within the country, more religious tolerance, broader base of reasonableness, over a period.

Dublin expands rapidly. Population shift from Belfast.

Greater unemployment and substantial business recession in the North.

A gradual movement towards accelerated fusion with Europe.

Better commercial decisions from Government with its hard-headed Northern involved.

Economic unity with U.K. a possibility.

Balance between industry and agriculture.

As a nation, the two parts together, effectively unified would make an excellent whole.

General raising of standards of public life e.g., South would raise its standards of Public Facilities to that of North and North would adopt better social facilities of South.

PROBLEM 9

Ireland is accepted to the Common Market on 10 July 1969. What would be the consequences for Ireland?

Enormous American Interest, common language, labor resources, space.

Property values start to jump.

We tend to lose ownership of our industry, but industrial tempo rises, standards of living improve.

Collapse of large segment of industry.

Transference in politics from cultural and nationalistic considerations to economic ones.

Immediate comparative prosperity for farmers.

Many industries would be ill-prepared and swamped out of business.

More contact with Continental Europe on all fronts—social, cultural and political—would remove the obsession with Ireland's past history *vis-à-vis* U.K.

Big influx of Irish managers into the IMI.

Increased prosperity to farmers in general and increased agricultural productivity.

Farmers should, not would, become the new rich.

Flooding of continental goods into shops.

More languages taught. Interchange of students.

Unemployed customs staff!

PROBLEM 10

A radical shift in climatic influences make Ireland's climate similar to that of Southern California. What would be the consequences?

Happier, smiling Irish people under sun and blue skies. (Grey skies bring grey minds.)

Not enough room on beaches for Irish and flood of foreign tourists.

We would become the market garden of Europe with great increase in prosperity.

Population would increase by about 1,000 a day through influx from U.K. and Europe, until Government would impose restrictions.

As a race, our temperament would improve to an unrecognizable degree.

No more sadness and mist that do be rising. Rather: optimism and more aggressiveness.

Replanning of cities taking emphasis off the solid concrete-brick towards lighter materials.

Disposition of people more optimistic.

Ireland would be Europe's playground.

The boys would go where the girls would be, on the beaches, and Americans would throng to us.

Elimination of major topic of conversation!

After a few years the country would be as brassy, overcrowded and intolerable as California is (or would be with only 350 x 150 miles to grow in).

GROUP DISCUSSION AND BRAINSTORMING

The results of the discussion and brainstorming sessions are extremely difficult to summarize, and they are particularly difficult to understand in any detail if one is not quite familiar with the Irish economy. Since this account of the research is not intended for use by those who might wish to apply the suggested innovations in the actual economic situation in Ireland, we shall content ourselves with a few very general categories of suggestion and give some examples under each category. Actually, a total of 824 discriminably different suggested innovations were produced by the four groups of managers. Each group worked on the problem for a total of three hours, the first two in discussion and the third in brainstorming. The brainstorming session, because of the rule discouraging criticism and argument, resulted in a great many more specific suggestions, and also many more zany ones; the discussion sessions, perhaps because of the social stature of the individuals involved, were rather slow-moving, with a certain, perhaps inevitable, amount of speechifying and position-taking. Once the positions were defined, however, the discussion loosened up somewhat, and finally the semi-play atmosphere induced by the brainstorming instructions seemed to clear the way for imaginative ideas which were not self-interested or role-consistent.

For purposes of illustration, we have selected 30 ideas from the brainstorming sessions and four of the most prominent themes in the group discussion. These we present with a minimum of comment, using as far as possible the actual phrasing of the participants.

Brainstorming

1. Hold a world's fair every five years.
2. Obtain access to N.Y. stock market.
3. Change to the Metric System.
4. Farm the ocean to encourage production of marine foods.
5. Change our national values to materialism.
6. Educate the civil servants to favor innovation.
7. Make it possible for people to make a contract to put a certain percent of his income into savings tax free.
8. More investment must be put into creation of merchandising, sales, and market research.
9. A "design college" is needed.
10. Develop chains of small hotels. Fifty rooms, women hired on retainer basis for care of five rooms each.
11. A high-level English-teaching summer school (foreign exchange would thus be brought in).
12. We need a national development corporation.
13. Start a national hydraulic lab—producing harbor models.
14. Start an African institute for civil service training.
15. Inland waterway development is needed.
16. Managers should teach in universities.
17. Provide an old age retirement inducement for American millionaires by reducing death benefits.
18. I wish to God they would stop teaching Irish.
19. More offshore sailing and cruising should be made available from seaside hotels.
20. Promote Ireland as a place for international conferences.
21. There's too much secrecy—we should learn to speak out.
22. Pay much more attention to the young and to encouraging talent; get rid of the old men.
23. Sabbaticals in industry for return to university training.
24. A better statistical office and more open publication of figures is necessary. Total market statistics should be published.
25. Change the income tax to increase incentive for the salaried employee.

26. People with good ideas but no capital should be able to get credit.

27. International exchange of personnel to stress the "romance of business."

28. Put a cruise liner on land.

29. Development of natural beauty around our coasts.

30. "We really must start with our youngsters in schools—living for Ireland rather than dying for Ireland—put their minds on the problems of development, change, and innovation."

Ideas Emerging from Group Discussion

1. The Irish universities should assume a much more active role in providing scientific and technological training of a sort that would support economic development. The ties between the universities and the business community should be more assiduously cultivated, and businessmen should take a more active initiative in this. University course offerings that would make it easier for managers to return to the university setting for specialized training courses that would keep them abreast of new technological, managerial, and scientific thinking throughout the world should be encouraged. Admission requirements should be made much more flexible for training courses leading to "qualification" for managerial functions. (It was pointed out in this connection that IMI research, subsequently reported in *The Management of Irish Industry,* showed that only one manager in three [a total of about 2000 managers in the country as a whole] was "academically qualified," that is, held either a university degree or a certificate from a professional training institute.)

This recognition by Irish managers of the importance of the universities in stimulating innovation in industry accords well with the recent conclusion of a special panel (the Panel on Invention and Innovation) appointed by the U. S. Department of Commerce, at the President's direction, to come up with answers to the question, "What can be done to improve the climate for technological innovation?" The panel, which included such key figures as Peter G. Peterson, president of Bell and Howell, Peter G.

Goldmark, president of CBS Laboratories, John F. Dessauer, executive vice-president for research and engineering at Xerox Corporation, and Dr. Robert A. Charpie, president of the Electronics Division of Union Carbide, considered proximity to a major university one of the most important factors in the development of innovative industries.

2. "Venture capital" should be much more freely available, and capital sources should have staffing that would enable them to appraise the feasibility of proposed developments based on ideas for technological innovation. (This appeared to be a sensitive point and since two of the discussion groups included, respectively, the present governor of the Bank of Ireland and his immediate predecessor, some stiff exchanges occurred when the particulars of this general point were considered.)

3. Freer trade agreements with the United Kingdom should be sought on a longer-term basis and with firmer commitments. The point emerged that the Irish fight for independence from England was achieved at considerable economic cost, quite apart from the loss of life and property in the war of independence and the subsequent civil war. There was obvious pride in independence, but at the same time a recognition of the genuine *interdependence* economically of Ireland and the United Kingdom.

4. The Irish educational system should be studied closely to see how it might be improved, particularly in terms of preparing students for further training in mathematics, science, and economics. A number of specific suggestions were made and vigorously debated; we cite a few of the controversial ones to give the general flavor of the discussions:
a. The power of the Catholic clergy in the school system should be reduced, and the management of the schools should be in the hands of laymen.
b. Free education should be extended from 6 years to 12. (It has subsequently been extended from 6 to 8.)

c. Industry and government should cooperate in establishing many more scholarships at the universities.

d. Salaries in education should be greatly improved so that capable members of the laity could consider teaching as a life career.

e. Special programs should be developed so that young people who are put to work early on the farms might still continue their education. Education by television should be developed by the government.

f. Adult education should be encouraged; adult workers, someone suggested, should have one paid day off per week to attend school.

The comments on education revealed an urgent sense of need for change in the school system. One discussant remarked, "We have a desperate shortage of educated people." Another said, "The government needs a big push." Still another: "All that Ireland really can produce is ideas, and you need education to put to use the brains we have in this country."

References

ADAMS, H. *The education of Henry Adams.* New York: Modern Library, 1931, pp. 11–14, 41–42.

ALLPORT, G. W. *Personality.* New York: Holt, Rinehart and Winston, 1937.

ANDREWS, E. Development of imagination in pre-school children. *University of Iowa Studies in Character,* 1930, **3**, 4.

BALZAC, H. DE. *Louis Lambert* and *Seraphita.* In Vol. 17 *Oeuvres,* 24 vols. Paris: Société d'éditions litteraires et artistiques, 1907.

BARRON, F. Originality in relation to personality and intellect. *Journal of Personality,* 1957, **25**, 730–742.

BARRON, F. The psychology of imagination. *Scientific American,* 1958, **199**, 151–166.

BARRON, F. Creativity. In A. Deutsch (Ed.), *The encyclopedia of mental health,* Vol. II. New York: F. Watts, 1963.

BARRON, F. *Creativity and psychological health.* Princeton, N. J.: Van Nostrand, 1963.

BARRON, F. Integration, diffusion, and enduring attention as aspects of the creative process. In R. W. White (Ed.), *The study of lives: Essays on personality in honor of Henry A. Murray.* New York: Atherton Press, 1963.

BARRON, F. Creativity and genius. In A. Deutsch (Ed.), *The encyclopedia of mental health.* New York: F. Watts, 1963.

BARRON, F.   The needs for order and disorder as motives in creative activity. In C. W. Taylor and F. Barron (Eds.), *Scientific Creativity*. New York: Wiley, 1963.

BARRON, F.   The psychology of creativity. In *Encyclopaedia Britannica*. New York: Encyclopaedia Britannica, Inc., 1963. Vol. 6, pp. 711–712.

BARRON, F.   *Creativity and personal freedom*. Princeton, N. J.: Van Nostrand, 1968.

BARRON, F. & EGAN, D.   Leaders and innovators in Irish management. *Journal of Management Studies*, 1968, **5** (1), 41–61.

BARRON, F., JARVIK, M. & BUNNELL, S.   The hallucinogenic drugs. *Scientific American*, April, 1964.

BARRON, F., & WELSH, G. S.   Artistic perception as a possible factor in personality style: Its measurement by figure preference test. *Journal of Psychology*, 1952, **33**, 199–203.

BENNETT, G. K.   *A test of productive thinking*. New York: Psychological Corporation, 1947.

BERDYAEV, N.   *Dostoevski: An interpretation*. (Trans. by Donald Attwatter.) New York: Sheed and Ward, 1934.

BERDYAEV, N.   *The meaning of the creative act*. (Trans. by D. A. Laurie.) New York: Harper & Row, 1954.

BLAKE, W.   The marriage of heaven and hell. In D. J. Sloss and J. P. R. Wallis (Eds.), *The prophetic writings of William Blake*, Vol. 1. Oxford: Clarendon Press, 1926.

BOWERS, P. G.   Effect of hypnosis and suggestions of reduced defensiveness on creativity text performance. *Journal of Personality*, 1967, **35** (2), 311–322.

BRIMHALL, D. R.   Family resemblances among American men of science. *American Naturalist*, 1923, **57**, 74–88.

BROWN, G. I.   An experiment in the teaching of creativity. *School Review*, 1965, **93**, 4.

BROWN, G. I.   A second study in the teaching of creativity. *Harvard Educational Review*, 1965, **35** (1), 39–54.

BURCHARD, E.   The use of projective techniques in the analysis of creativity. *Journal of Projective Techniques*, 1952, **16**, 412–427.

CANDOLLE, A. DE.   *Histoire des sciences et des savants depuis deux siècles*. Genève: Georg, 1885.

CATTELL, J. McK.   A statistical study of eminent men. *Popular Science Monthly*, February 1903, 359–377.

CATTELL, R. B.   The personality and motivation of the researcher from measurements of contemporaries and from biography. In C. W. Taylor and F. Barron (Eds.), *Scientific creativity*. New York: Wiley, 1963.

CATTELL, R. B. & DREVDAHL, J. E. A comparison of the personality profile of eminent researchers with that of eminent teachers and administrators and that of the general population. *British Journal of Psychology*, 1955, 46, 248–261.

CLARKE, E. L. *American men of letters: their nature and nurture.* New York: Columbia University Press, 1916.

COVINGTON, M. V., & CRUTCHFIELD, R. S. Experiments in the use of programed instruction for the facilitation of creative problem solving. *Programed Instruction*, January 1965.

COX, C. The early mental traits of 300 geniuses. *Genetic Studies of Genius*, Vol. II. Stanford: Stanford University Press, 1926.

CRUTCHFIELD, R. S. Assessment of persons through a quasi-group interaction technique. *Journal of Abnormal and Social Psychology*, 1951, 4, 577–588.

DEARBORN, G. V. A study of imagination. *American Journal of Psychology*, 1898, 5 (9), 183.

DREWS, E. Freedom to grow. *N. E. A. Journal*, September 1960, 49 (6), 20–22.

ELLIS, H. *A study of British genius.* London: Hurst and Blackett, 1904.

FLANAGAN, J. Definition and measurement of ingenuity. In C. W. Taylor and F. Barron (Eds.), *Scientific creativity.* New York: Wiley, 1963.

FREUD, S. Dostoevski and parricide. (Trans. by D. F. Tait.) In *Collected papers.* London: Hogarth, 1952. Vol. V, pp. 222–232.

GALTON, F. *English men of science: Their nature and nurture.* London: Macmillan, 1874.

GALTON, F. *Hereditary genius.* London: Macmillan, 1925.

GALTON, F. *Inquiries into human faculty.* London: Macmillan, 1883.

GETZELS, J. W., & JACKSON, P. O. *Creativity and intelligence.* New York: Wiley, 1962.

GETZELS, J. W., & JACKSON, P. O. Occupational choice and cognitive functions. Career aspirations of the highly intelligent and the highly creative adolescent. *Journal of Abnormal and Social Psychology*, 1960, 61, 119–123.

GOERTZEL, V., and GOERTZEL, M. G. *Cradles of eminence.* Boston: Little Brown, 1962.

GORDON, W. J. J. *Synectics: The development of creative capacity.* New York: Harper & Row, 1961.

GOUGH, H. G. Techniques for identifying the creative research scientist. In D. W. MacKinnon (Ed.), *The creative person.* Berkeley: University of California Extension, 1961.

GOUGH, H. G. The Adjective Check List as a personality assessment research technique. *Psychological Reports, Monograph Supplement*, 1960, 6, 107–122.

GOUGH, H. G., & WOODWORTH, D. G. Stylistic variations among professional research scientists. *Journal of Psychology*, 1960, **49**, 87–98.

GUILFORD, J. P. Creativity. *American Psychologist*, 1950, **5**, 444–454.

GUILFORD, J. P. Factorial angles to psychology. *Psychological Review*, 1961, **68**, 1–20.

GUILFORD, J. P. Factor analysis in a test-development program. *Psychological Review*, 1948, **55**, 79–94.

HALL, W. B. The development of a technique for assessing aesthetic predisposition and its application to a sample of research scientists. Paper read at Western Psychological Association, Monterey, California, April 1958. Berkeley: Institute of Personality Assessment and Research, University of California.

HAMMER, E. F. *Creativity*. New York: Random House, 1961.

HEIDEGGER, M. *What is metaphysics?* Bonn: F. Cohen, 1929.

HELSON, R. Creativity, sex, and mathematics. In D. W. MacKinnon (Ed.), *The creative person*. Berkeley: University of California Extension, 1961.

HELSON, R. Personality characteristics and developmental history of creative college women. *Genetic Psychology Monographs*, 1967, **76**, 205–256.

HOLLAND, J. L., & KENT, L. The concentration of scholarship funds and its implications for education. *College and University*, Summer 1960, **35** (4), 471–483.

HUXLEY, A. *The doors of perception* and *Heaven and hell*. New York: Harper & Row, 1964.

JUNG, C. G. *Psychological types*. New York:. Harcourt, 1924.

KUBIE, L. S. *Neurotic distortion of the creative process*. Lawrence, Kansas: University of Kansas Press, 1958.

LAWRENCE, D. H. *Psychoanalysis and the unconscious* and *Fantasia of the unconscious*. Melbourne: W. Heinemann, 1961.

MACKINNON, D. W. The nature and nurture of creative talent. *American Psychologist*, 1962, 484–495.

MACKINNON, D. W., et al. *Proceedings of the Conference on "The Creative Person,"* University of California Alumni Center, Lake Tahoe, California. Berkeley: University of California Extension, 1961.

MARITAIN, J. *Creative intuition in art and poetry*. New York: Meridian, 1955.

MCCARTHY, M. *The group*. New York: Harcourt, 1963.

MCCLOY, W., & MEIER, N. C. Re-creative imagination. *Psychological Monographs*, 1931, **51** (5), 108–116.

MCWHINNIE, H. J. A study of the relationships between figure preferences for complexity-asymmetry and preference in works of art in fourth-, fifth, and sixth-grade children. *Scientia Paedagogica Experimentalis,* 1967, 4 (2), 209–230.

MEDNICK, S. The associative basis of the creative process. *Psychological Review,* 1962, 69, 220–232.

MEER, B., & STEIN, M. I. Measures of intelligence and creativity. *Journal of Psychology,* 1955, 39, 117–126.

MURRAY, H. A. *Explorations in personality.* New York: Oxford, 1938.

MURRAY, H. A., & CHRISTENSEN, P. R. *The Thematic Apperception Test manual.* Cambridge, Mass.: Harvard University Press, 1943.

MURRAY, H. A., MACKINNON, D. W., MILLER, J. G., FISKE, D. W., & HANFMANN, E. *Assessment of Men.* Reissue. New York: Holt, Rinehart and Winston, 1963.

ODIN, A. Genèse des grands hommes. *Gens des lettres francais modernes.* Paris, 1895.

OSBORN, A. F. *Applied imagination.* New York: Scribner, 1957.

PARNES, S. J. Do you really understand brainstorming? In S. J. Parnes and H. F. Harding (Eds.), *A source book for creative thinking.* New York: Scribner, 1962.

REXROTH, K. The vivisection of a poet. *The Nation,* 1957, 185 (20), 450–453.

ROE, A. *The making of a scientist.* New York: Dodd, Mead, 1952.

RORSCHACH, H. *Psychodiagnostics.* Bern: Huber (Grune & Stratton, New York, distributors), 1942.

SCHNEIDMAN, E. S. Orientations toward death. In. R. W. White (Ed.), *The study of lives.* New York: Atherton, 1963.

SIMPSON, R. M. Creative imagination. *American Journal of Psychology,* 1922, 33, 23–35.

STAFFORD, P. G., & GOLIGHTLY, B. H. *LSD: The problem-solving psychedelic.* New York: Award Books, 1967.

SWEDENBORG, E. *Heaven and hell.* London: The Swedenborg Society, 1850.

TAYLOR, C. W., & BARRON, F. *Scientific creativity: Its recognition and development.* New York: Wiley, 1963.

TAYLOR, C. W., BERRY, P. C., & BLOCK, C. H. Does group participation when using brainstorming facilitate or inhibit creative thinking? ONR Technical Memorandum, Psychology Department, Yale University, 1957.

TERMAN, L. M. The intelligence quotient of Francis Galton in childhood. *American Journal of Psychology,* 1917, 28, 204–215.

THURSTONE, L. L. Creative talent. In L. L. Thurstone (Ed.), *Applications of psychology.* New York: Harper & Row, 1952.

TORRANCE, E. P.   *Guiding creative talent.* Englewood, N. J.: Prentice-Hall, 1962.

TORRANCE, E. P.   The Minnesota studies of creative behavior: National and international extensions. *The Journal of Creative Behavior,* 1967, 1 (2), 137–154.

VISHER, S. S.   *Scientists starred in American men of science, 1903–1943.* Baltimore: The Johns Hopkins Press, 1947.

WELCH, L.   Recombination of ideas in creative thinking. *Journal of Applied Psychology,* 1946, 30, 638–643.

WERTHEIMER, M.   *Productive thinking.* New York: Harper & Row, 1954.

WHITE, R. W.   *The study of lives.* New York: Atherton, 1963.

WOODS, F. A.   *Mental and moral heredity in royalty.* New York: Holt. Rinehart and Winston, 1906.

WOOLF, V.   *Orlando.* New York: Harcourt, 1928.

WOOLF, V.   *A room of one's own.* London: Hogarth, 1935.

Selected Bibliography

ANDERSON, H. H. *Creativity and its cultivation.* New York: Harper, 1959.

ARNHEIM, L. Perceptual abstraction and art. *Psychological Review,* 1947, **54,** 66–82.

ASCH, S. E. *Social psychology.* Englewood Cliffs, N.J.: Prentice-Hall, 1952.

BALINT, M. The three areas of the mind. *International Journal of Psychological Analysis,* 1958, 39, 328–340.

BALKAN, E. R. & MASSERMAN, J. H. Language of phantasy, III. *Journal of Psychology,* 1940, 10, 75–86.

BARRON, F. Inventory of personal philosophy. Berkeley: University of California, 1952.

BARRON, F. Personality style and perceptual choice. *Journal of Personality,* 1952, **20,** 385–401.

BARRON, F. Complexity-simplicity as a personality dimension. *Journal of Abnormal and Social Psychology,* 1953, 68, 163–172.

BARRON, F. Some personality correlates of independence of judgment. *Journal of Personality,* 1953, 21, 289–297.

BARRON, F. The disposition toward originality. *Journal of Abnormal and Social Psychology,* 1955, **51,** 478–485.

BARRON, F. The word rearrangement test. Maxwell Air Force Base, Alabama: Officer Education Research Laboratory, May, 1955. (*Technical Memorandum OERL-TM-55-11.*)

BARRON, F.   Threshold for the perception of human movement in inkblots. *Journal of Consulting Psychology*, 1955, **19**, 33–38.

BARRON, F., GUILFORD, J. P., CHRISTENSEN, P. R., BERGER, R. M., & KETT-NER, N. W.   Interrelations of various measures of creative traits. *Technical Memorandum AF18(600)-8.* Berkeley, California: Institute of Personality Assessment and Research, 1957.

BARTLETT, F. C.   Types of imagination. *Journal of Psychological Studies,* 1928, **3**, 78–85.

BELLAK, L.   Creativity: Some random notes to a systematic consideration. *Journal of Projective Techniques,* 1958, **22**, 363–380.

BERES, D.   Perception, imagination and reality. *International Journal of Psychoanalysis,* 1960, **41**, 327–334.

BERES D.   The psychoanalytic psychology of imagination. *Journal of the American Psychoanalytical Association,* 1960, **8**, 252–269.

BERGER, R. M., GUILFORD, J. P., & CHRISTENSEN, P. R.   A factor-analytical study of planning abilities. *Psychological Monographs,* 1957, **71**, (Whole No.. 435).

BERGSON, H.   *The creative mind.* New York: Philosophical Library, 1946.

BISCHLER, W.   Intelligence and the higher mental functions. (Trans. by P. Winner.) *Psychoanalytic Quarterly,* 1937, **6**, 277–307.

BLATT, S. J., & STEIN, M. T.   Some personality, value and cognitive characteristics of the creative person. *American Journal of Psychology,* 1957, **12**, 406.

BOWERMAN, W. G.   *Studies in genius.* New York: Philosophical Library, 1947.

BRITTAIN, W. L.   A study of imagination. *Pedagogical Seminary,* 1907, **14**, 137–207.

BRITTAIN, W., & BEITTAL, K.   Analyses of levels of creative performance. *Journal of Aesthetics and Art Criticism,* 1960, **19**, 83–90.

BUELL, W. D.   Validity of behavioral rating scale items for assessment of individual creativity. *Journal of Applied Psychology,* 1960, **44**, 407–412.

BURKHART, R.   The relation of intelligence to artistic ability. *Journal of Aesthetics and Art Criticism,* 1958, **12**, 230–241.

BURT, C.   The structure of the mind: A review of the results of factor analysis. *British Journal of Educational Psychology,* 1949, **19**, 100–111, 176–199.

CAMPBELL, D. T.   Blind variation and selective retentions in creative thought as in other human knowledge processes. *Psychological Review,* 1960, **67**, 380–400.

CARROLL, J. B.   A factor analysis of verbal abilities. *Psychometrika,* 1941, **6**, 279–307.

CHAMBERS, J. A.   Relating personality and biographical factors to scientific creativity. *Psychological Monographs,* 78, 7, 1964.

CHRISTENSEN, P. R., & GUILFORD, J. P.   An experimental study of verbal fluency factors. *British Journal of Statistical Psychology,* 1963, 16, 1–26.

CRAWFORD, P. R.   *Techniques of creative thinking.* New York: Hawthorn, 1954.

CRUTCHFIELD, R. S.   Conformity and character. *American Psychologist,* 1955, 10, 191–198.

CRUTCHFIELD, R. S.   Conformity and creative thinking. In H. E. Gruber, G. Terrell, and M. Wertheimer (Eds.), *Contemporary approaches to creative thinking.* New York: Atherton Press, 1962.

CRUTCHFIELD, R. S.   Independent thought in a conformist world. In S. M. Farber and R. H. L. Wilson (Eds.), *Conflict and creativity.* New York: McGraw-Hill, 1963.

CRUTCHFIELD, R. S., & COVINGTON, M. V.   Programed instruction in creativity. *Programed Instruction,* 1965, IV, 4, 1–8.

DAVENPORT, C. B.   *Naval officers: Their heredity and development.* Washington: Carnegie Institute, 1919.

DAVIS, P. C.   A factor analysis of the Wechler-Bellevue scale. *Educational and Psychological Measurement,* 1956, 14, 127–146.

DREVDAHL, J. E.   Factors of importance for creativity. *Journal of Clinical Psychology,* 1956, 12, 21–26.

DREVDAHL, J. E., & CATTELL, R. B.   Personality and creativity in artists and writers. *Journal of Clinical Psychology,* 1958, 14, 107–111.

EIDUSON, B. L.   Artist and non-artist: A comparative study. *Journal of Personnel,* 1958, 26, 13–28.

EYSENCK, H. J.   *Dimensions of personality.* London: Routledge, 1947.

EYSENCK, H. J.   *The structure of personality.* New York: Wiley, 1953.

FLEMING, E. S., & WEINTRAUB, S.   Additional rigidity as a measure of creativity in gifted children. *Journal of Educational Psychology,* 1962, 53, 81–85.

FRICK, J. W., GUILFORD, J. P. CHRISTENSEN, P. R., & MERRIFIELD, P. R.   A factor analytic study of creative thinking. *Educational and Psychological Measurement,* 1959, 19, 469–496.

GARDNER, J.   *Self-renewal.* New York: Harper & Row, 1963.

GHISELIN, B.   *The creative process.* Berkeley: University of California Press, 1952.

GIOVACCHINI, P. L.   On scientific creativity. *Journal of the American Psychoanalytical Association* 1960, 8, 407–476.

GLASS, S. I.   Creative thinking can be released and applied. *Personality Journal,* 1960, 39, 176, 177.

GOUGH, H. G. *Manual for the California Psychological Inventory.* Palo Alto, Calif.: Consulting Psychologists Press, 1957.

GOUGH, H. G. *Manual for the Adjective Checklist.* Palo Alto, Calif.: Consulting Psychologists Press, 1965.

GREENACRE, P. The childhood of the artist. Libidinal phase development and greatness. *The psychoanalytic study of the child.* Vol. XII. New York: International Universities Press, 1957. Pp. 47–72.

GRIFFIN, D. P. Movement responses and creativity. *Journal of Consulting Psychology,* 1958, **22**, 134–136.

GUILFORD, J. P. Structure of intellect. *Psychological Bulletin,* 1956, **53**, 267–293.

GUILFORD, J. P. Creative abilities in the arts. *Psychological Review,* 1957, **64**, 110–118.

GUILFORD, J. P. *Personality.* New York: McGraw-Hill, 1959, 382, 383.

GUILFORD, J. P. Three faces of intellect. *American Psychologist,* 1959, **14**, 469–479.

GUILFORD, J. P. Basic conceptual problems in the psychology of thinking. *Annals of the New York Academy of Science,* 1960, **91**, 6–21.

GUILFORD, J. P. Frontiers in thinking teachers should know about. *Reading Teacher,* 1960, **13**, 176–182.

GUILFORD, J. P. Progress in the discovery of intellectual factors. In C. W. Taylor (Ed.), *Widening horizons in creativity.* New York: McGraw-Hill, 1964.

GUILFORD, J. P. Zero correlations among tests of intellectual abilities. *Psychological Bulletin,* 1964 (6), 61.

GUTMAN, H. Biological roots of creativity. *Genetic Psychology Monographs,* 1961, **64**, 417–458.

HALBECK, C. R. The creative personality. *American Journal of Psychoanalysis,* 1945, **5**, 49–58.

HARMS, E. A test for types of formal creativity. *Psychological Bulletin,* 1939, **36**, 526, 527.

HARRIS, D. Development and validity of test of creativity in engineering. *Journal of Applied Psychology,* 1960, **44**, 254–257.

HATHAWAY, S. R., & MCKINLEY, J. C. *Manual for the Minnesota Multiphasic Personality Inventory.* Minneapolis: University of Minnesota Press, 1943

HENRY, W. E. *The analysis of fantasy.* New York: Wiley, 1956.

HILGARD, E. R. Creativity and problem solving. In H. H. Anderson (Ed.), *Creativity and its cultivation.* New York: Harper, 1959. Pp. 162–180.

HUTCHINSON, E. D. Materials for the study of creative thinking. *Psychological Bulletin,* 1931, **28**, 392–410.

HUTTON, E., & BASSET, M. The effect of leucotomy on the creative personality. *Journal of Mental Science,* 1948, **94,** 333–380.

JOHNSON, S. R., & GLAZE, E. E. A critical analysis of psychological treatments of children's drawings and paintings. *Journal of Aesthetic and Art Criticism,* 1958, **17,** 242–250.

KETTNER, N. W., GUILFORD, J. P., & CHRISTENSEN, P. R. A factor-analytic study across the domains of reasoning, creativity, and evaluation. *Psychological Monographs,* 1959, **73,** (Whole No. 479).

KNAPP, R. H., & GOODRICH, H. B. *Origins of American scientists.* Chicago: University of Chicago Press, 1952.

KRIS, E. *Psychoanalytic exploration in art.* New York: International Universities Press, 1952.

LEHMAN, H. C. *Age and achievement.* Princeton, N. J.: Princeton University Press, 1953.

LEVY, N. Notes on the creative process and the creative person. *Psychiatric Quarterly,* 1961, **35,** 66–77.

MACKINNON, D. W. Fact and fancy in personality research. *American Psychologist,* 1953, **8,** 138–146.

MACKINNON, D. W. Genus architectus creator varietas Americanus. *American Institute of Architects Journal,* September 1960, 31–35.

MACKINNON, D. W. Fostering creativity in students of engineering. *Journal of Engineering Education,* 1961, **52,** 129–142.

MALTZMAN, I., SIMON, S., RASKIN, D., & LICHT, L. Experimental studies in the training of originality. *Psychological Monographs,* 1960, **74,** (6), 1–23.

MANDELL, M. M., & ADAMS, S. Measuring originality in physical scientists. *Educational and Psychological Measurement,* 1948, **8,** 515–582.

MARKEY, F. V. Imagination. *Psychological Bulletin,* 1935, **32,** 212–236.

MASLOW, A. H. Creativity in self-actualizing people. In H. H. Anderson (Ed.), *Creativity and its cultivation.* New York: Harper, 1959. Chap. 7.

MASLOW, A. H. Defense and growth. *Merrill-Palmer Quarterly,* 1956, **3,** 37, 38.

MAY, R. The nature of creativity. In. H. H. Anderson (Ed.), *Creativity and its cultivation.* New York: Harper, 1959.

MCGEOCH, J. A. Relationship between three tests for imagination and their correlation with intelligence. *Journal of Applied Psychology,* 1924, **8,** 443–459.

MOONEY, R. L. A conceptual model for integrating four approaches to the identification of creative talent. In C. W. Taylor and F. Barron (Eds.), *Scientific creativity.* New York: Wiley, 1963.

MOSING, L. W.　Development of a multi-media creativity test. *Dissertation Abstracts*, 1959, **19**, 2137.

MUELLER, R. E.　*Inventivity.* New York: John Day, 1963.

MULLINS, C. J.　Selection of creative personnel. *Personnel Journal*, 1960, **39**, 12, 13.

MUNSTERBERG, E., & MUSSEN, P. H.　Personality structure of art students. *Journal of Personality*, 1953, **21**, 457–466.

MURPHY, G.　Creativeness. *Menninger Quarterly*, 1957, **11**, 1–6.

MYERS, I. B.　*Some findings with regard to type and manual for Myers-Briggs Type Indicator, Form E.* Swarthmore, Pa.: Author, 1958.

NISBET, R. A., & BLISTEN, D.　The creative context: A preface. *Autonomous Groups Bulletin*, 1957, **12**, 1–3.

OROWAN, E.　Our universities and scientific creativity. *Bulletin of Atomic Science*, 1959, **6**, 2369.

OSTWALD, W.　*Grosse Manner.* Liepzig: Akademische Verlagsgesellschaft, 1909.

OWENS, W. A., SCHUMACHER, C. F., & CLARK, J. B.　The measurement of creativity in machine design. *Journal of Applied Psychology*, 1957, **41**, 297–302.

PARNES, S. J.　Effects of brain-storming instructions on creative problem-solving. *Journal of Educational Psychology*, 1959, **50**, 171–176.

PARNES, S. J., & MEADOW, A.　Evaluation of persistence of effects produced by a creative problem-solving course. *Psychological Reports*, 1960, **7**, 357–361.

PETERSON, R. O.　*Creativity and conformity: A problem of organization.* Foundation for research on human behavior. Ann Arbor, Michigan, 1958.

PHRATOL, P.　Experimental study of creativity and intelligence and school achievement. *Psychological Studies* (Mysore), 1962, **7**, 1–9.

PIAGET, P.　*The psychology of intelligence.* New York: Harcourt, 1950.

PIERS, G. V., & DANIELS, J. M.　The identification of creativity in adolescence. *Journal of Educational Psychology*, 1960, **51**, 346–357.

PINE, F.　Thematic drive content and creativity. *Journal of Personality*, 1959, **27**, 136–151.

PINE, F., & HOH, R.　Creativity and the primary process: A study of adaptive regression. *Journal of Abnormal Psychology*, 1960, **61**, 370–379.

PORTNOY, J.　Is the creative process similar in the arts? *Journal of Aesthetics and Art Criticism*, 1960, **19**, 191–195.

REES, M. E., & GOLDMAN, M.　Some relationships between creativity and personality. *Journal of Genetic Psychology*, 1961, **65**, 145–161.

RHODES, J. M.　The dynamics of creativity: An interpretation of literature on creativity with a proposed procedure for objective research. *Dissertation Abstracts*, 1957, **17**, 96.

RIVLIN, L. G. Creativity and the self-attitudes and socialization of high school students. *Journal of Educational Psychology,* 1959, **60**, 147–152.

ROBERTS, W. Normal and abnormal depersonalization. *Journal of Mental Science,* 1960, **106**, 478–493.

ROE, A. Artists and their work. *Journal of Personality,* 1946, **15**, 1–40.

ROE, A. The personality of artists. *Educational Psychology,* 1946, **6**, 401–408.

ROE, A. Painting and personality. *Rorschach Research Exchange,* 1946, **10**, 81–100.

ROE, A. A psychological examination of eminent biologists. *Journal of Consulting Psychology,* 1949, **13**, 225–246.

ROE, A. A psychological study of eminent biologists. *Psychological Monographs,* 1951, **54** (14), 68 pp.

ROE, A. A study of imagery in research scientists. *Journal of Personality,* 1951, **19**, 459–470.

ROE, A. Psychological tests of research scientists. *Journal of Consulting Psychology,* 1951, **15**, 491–495.

ROE, A. A psychological study of eminent psychologists and anthropologists, and a comparison with biologists and physical scientists. *Psychological Monographs,* 1953, **57** (2), 55 pp.

ROSEN, V. H. Some aspects of the role of imagination in psychoanalysis. *Journal of the American Psychoanalytic Association,* 1960, **8**, 229–251.

RUTHERFORD, J. M. Personality correlates of creativity. *Dissertation Abstracts,* 1960, **20**, 4434.

SCHACHTEL, E. G. *Metamorphosis: On the development of affect, perception and memory.* New York: Basic Books, 1959.

SCHINER, J. Free association and ego formation in creativity. *American Imago,* 1960, **17**, 61–74.

SIMONS, J. H. Scientific research in universities. *American Scientist,* 1960, **48**, 80–90.

SPOERL, D. T. Personality and drawing in retarded children. *Character and Personality,* 1940, **8**, 227–239.

SPRECHER, T. B. An investigation of criteria for creativity in engineers. *Dissertation Abstracts,* 1958, **18**, 1101, 1102.

STEIN, M. I. Creativity and culture. *Journal of Psychology,* 1953, **36**, 311–322.

STEIN, M. I., & MEER, B. Perceptual organization in a study of creativity. *Journal of Psychology,* 1954, **37**, 39–43.

STEIN, M. I., & HEINZE, S. J. *Creativity and the individual.* New York: Free Press, 1960.

STERN, W.   Cloud pictures. A new method for testing imagination. *Character and Personality*, 1937, **6**, 132–146.

STRONG, E. K., JR.   *The vocational interests of men and women.* Stanford: Stanford University Press, 1943.

TAYLOR, C. W.   The identification of creative scientific talent. *American Psychologist*, 1959, **14**, 100–102.

TAYLOR, I. A.   The nature of the creative process. In P. Smith (Ed.), *Creativity*. New York: Hastings, 1959. Pp. 51–82.

TERMAN, L. M., & ODIN, M. H.   *The gifted child grows up.* Vol. 4, *Genetic Studies of Genius*. Stanford, California: Stanford University Press, 1947.

THURSTONE, L. L.   Primary mental abilities. *Psychometric Monographs*, No. 1, 1938.

TORRANCE, E. P.   Current research on creativity. *Journal of Consulting Psychology*, 1959, **6**, 309–316.

TORRANCE, E. P.   Explorations in creative thinking. *Education*, 1960, **81**, 216–220.

TORRANCE, E. P.   Problems of the highly gifted child. *Gifted Child Quarterly*, 1961, **5**, 31–34.

TRUE, G. H.   Creativity as a function of ideational fluency, practicability and specific training. *Dissertation Abstracts*, 1957, **17**, 402.

VERNON, P. E.   *The structure of human abilities.* New York: Wiley, 1950.

VINACKE, W. E.   Creative thinking. In W. E. Vinacke (Ed.), *The psychology of thinking*. New York: McGraw-Hill, 1952. Pp. 238–261.

WALLAS, G.   *The art of thought.* New York: Harcourt, 1926.

WEISBERG, P. S., & SPRINGER, K.   Environmental factors in creative functioning of gifted children. *Archives of General Psychiatry*, 1961, **5**, 554–564.

WEISSMAN, P.   Development and creativity in actor and playwright. *Psychoanalytic Quarterly*, 1961, **30**, 638–643.

WENKART, A.   Modern art and human development. *American Journal of Psychoanalysis*, 1960, **20**, 174–179.

WHITING, C. S.   *Creative thinking.* New York: Holt, Rinehart and Winston, 1958.

WILSON, R. C., GUILFORD, J. P., & CHRISTENSEN, P. R.   The measurement of individual differences in originality. *Psychological Bulletin*, 1953, **50**, 362–370.

WILSON, R. N.   Poetic creativity, process and personality. *Psychiatry*, 1954, **17**, 163–176.

Name Index

Subject Index